WINGS OVER THE JUNGLE

THE BRAZILIAN AIR FORCE IN THE AMAZON

Foreword: Lieutenant-General Carlos de Almeida Baptista – Copyright © 2000
Edition and Text: Carlos Lorch - Copyright © 2000
Graphic Designer: João Augusto S. Rodrigues
Maps: Alexandre Argozino Neto
Copydesk: Heloísa Mesquita Portes
Photography
Wagner Ziegelmeyer/Action Editora – pages 15, 83, 87, 90, 112, 117, 128/129, 136/137, 142/143, cover (bottom photo)
Alexandre Durão/Action Editora – pages 8, 10, 14, 16/17, 74, 78, 84/85, 88/89, 98, 118/119, 120/121, 123, 132/133, 135, 138/139, back cover
Luiz Eduardo Perez/CCSIVAM – pages 12/13, 22/23, 30, 32/33, 35, 36/37, 39, 42/43, 92/93, 96/97, 100/101, 102, 106/107, 109, 114/115, 124/125, 140/141, 144
Domingos Peixoto – pages 46/47
Antônio Ricieri Biasus – pages 80/81, 130
J. M. Monteiro – pages 4/5, 6/7, 61,64, 67 cover (top photo)
Museu Aeroespacial – pages 48, 50, 51, 52/53, 55, 56, 63, 68, 71
Museu Paulista da USP – pages 21, 26, 27, 28
Museu do Índio – page 29
Biblioteca Nacional – pages 18, 24 (bottom photo), 25
Goethe Institut – page 24 (top photo)
Archivo del Museo de História Militar via Antonio Luis Sapienza Fracchia – pages 2/3
COMARA – Comissão dos Aeroportos da Amazônia – pages 72/73, 76/77
CCSIVAM – page 127
INPE – page 105 and endpapers

Country flight!

(Pages 2/3) The Airmail Service arrives at Asuncion in a cloud of dust! A WACO CJC takes off from the Paraguayan capital. This was the CAM's first international line. (Pages 4/5) Jungle Cat. During several years, the PBY-5A Catalinas of the Correio Aéreo Nacional da Amazônia allowed frontier posts, religious missions and Indian villages hidden in the depths of the jungle to survive. Capable of landing on the rivers, they were the only aircraft that could reach the more inaccessible corners of the Amazon Basin. (Pages 6/7) Bought in large numbers at the end of World War II, Douglas C-47 transports marked a new era in Airmail Service operations. Despite the fact that they were much larger and faster then the little WACOs and Beechcrafts, passengers still suffered with the long distances that separate the Amazon from the rest of the country. A flight from Rio de Janeiro to Belém took over nine hours, besides four stops, which made the trip last an entire day. The alternative, however, were ships that took a month to cover the same distance. (Pages 12/13) In the most inhospitable region of Brazil, where few dare to go, the wings of the Brazilian Air Force carry progress, integration, solace and presence.

L865

Lorch, Carlos.
    Wings Over the Jungle: The Brazilian Air Force in the Amazon /
Carlos Lorch; [illustrations: Alexandre Argozino Neto].
– Rio de Janeiro: Aerospace, 2000.
144 p. : il. ; 30 cm.

ISBN 85-87975-02-1

1. Brazil. Força Aérea Brasileira. 2. Amazon – Defense. I. Title

CDD-358.4147811

Realizado com incentivo da Lei 8313
de 23 de dezembro de 1991.
Lei de Incentivo à Cultura – Ministério da Cultura

LEI DE
INCENTIVO
À CULTURA

MINISTÉRIO
DA CULTURA

Printed in China

Aerospace Marketing e Publicidade Ltda.
Av. Churchill 129 Gr. 1004-parte
Centro – Rio de Janeiro, RJ
CEP – 20020- 050

CARLOS LORCH

WINGS OVER THE JUNGLE
THE BRAZILIAN AIR FORCE IN THE AMAZON

Aerospace

2000

*"To the men of the Brazilian Air Force
who integrated the vast Amazon."*

FOREWORD

The Amazon Jungle, which was once considered impenetrable, is seen today as a mighty system in its continental immensity, fascinating in flora and fauna, and coveted for her several resources and her potential for the future.

Since the Discovery of the New Continent, explorers have endeavored to unveil the mysteries of the largest forest in the World. The challenges were many, although few brought to light by historians. The anonymous efforts of these adventurers were kept alive into the present, mostly, by the wings of the Air Force.

In our days, our most intimate emotions are moved by the view of our flag flying in the wind at places that are only accessible after hours of flying over the fascinating green sea. This presence, we owe to the skill and creativity of men, who despite all existing obstacles, and the technological limitations of their time, were imbued with a dream, and have traced with their sweat, the frontiers of this Nation.

Today, new Explorers of the Skies continue the saga, transporting hope, and the certainty that we are building a better Brazil for our children.

This book, brought to you by the Air Force Command and made possible by Embraer, allows the reader an unmatched view of the past, the present and the future of the Brazilian Air Force in its mission to integrate and preserve the Amazon Region. It tells the story of the arduous work of the Men in Blue who challenged, integrated and are still laboring to defend the Brazilian Amazon.

Lieutenant-General Carlos de Almeida Baptista
Air Force Commander

FIVE HUNDRED YEARS OF EXPEDITIONS
THE DISCOVERY OF THE AMAZON

The first European to set eyes over the mighty Amazon was Vicente Yañez Pinzón who first sailed the mouth of the great river on the same year that Pedro Alvares Cabral landed on the coast of Bahia, officially discovering Brazil for the Portuguese Crown. However, this first approach to this most voluminous of the Planet's rivers is misleading as it was not from the Atlantic that the Amazon was first explored, rather from the distant Andean Altiplano, then the hotbed of Conquistador activity. In December 1540, Gonzalo Pizarro and his cousin, Gene-ral Francisco de Orellana, two intrepid Spaniard explo-rers each set foot from two different directions; Quito in the high Andes and Quayaquil, on the humid coast. Their objectives were the lands that lay on the other sides of the vast Cordillera. Their eyes were set on fields covered with cinnamon trees, then a resource as lusted as gold.

The expedition led by Pizarro left Quito on a southeasterly route, his men forming a long procession composed of some 350 Spaniards leading 4.000 Indian porters, two thousand llamas, another 2.000 hogs and yet another two thousand hounds trained to attack any hostile Indians they might find on their way. When the expedition finally reached the jungle on the eastern foothills of the Cordillera, over a hundred of the porters had perished. Orellana, who had left Quayaquil a few days later with a smaller group also endured the perils of the treacherous trek. Upon finally catching up with his cousin in the dark and humid rainforest, he led no more that 21 of his men, the rest having fallen along the way. They had advanced but 150 kilometers since the outset

For several centuries Brazilians lives in a thin strip of land along the coast. Only sporadically was the country's interior explored.

of their respective journeys. Seventy days later, at the head of an advanced party, Pizarro discovered a small river that ran for some 100 kilometers before flowing into another, considerably larger one. According to Friar Carbajal, whose writings survived the trip, the Spaniards decided to build a small brig with which they intended to explore downstream. Soon, the small boat escorted by 16 dugouts seized from local Indians, set sail down the river, the rest of the party carrying their supplies along the banks. On December 26, 1541 the situation began deteriorating. The river seemed endless, the hogs had practically all been consumed and the expedition had almost run out of food. Orellana picked 60 men and decided to push on downriver in search of food. It did not take long for Pizarro to understand that his cousin would not return. After eating the dogs and the horses, and feeling betrayed, Pizarro's men turned about and began the arduous march back to Quito. It would take them six months to reach the Altiplano.

Meanwhile, Orellana sailed down the great river. According to Carbajal's log the currents were so strong that turning back was impossible. Besides, the total lack of life on the riverbanks prompted the Spaniards to continue eastwards. Soon scattered Indian villages began to appear and believing he was near the mouth of the river, Orellana decided to abandon his canoes and build a second brig. With two larger boats the Spaniards gained speed on their eastward journey and in no time were battling the local tribes and capturing ample amounts of supplies with which to continue on their way. At this point they were near the dark waters of the Negro River. It was here that they first saw the fierce local women who fought courageously alongside their men. Influenced by ancient

European lore about the existence of the Amazons, Orellana's men believed they had finally reached their lands, Carbajal wasting no time in describing this unimaginable discovery. Thus began the myth of the existence of the Amazons, which would eventually name the entire region. It was during one of the battles with the Indians of the upper Negro that one of Orellana's men died, scarce seconds after being grazed by an Indian arrow. Europeans had witnessed curare for the first time.

In July 1542, the two boats finally arrived at the island of Marajó, not far from the mouth of the great river. They had sailed past the Portuguese settlement of Pará without having seen it. As one of the boats hit a log and foundered on the deep tan waters, the Spaniards were forced to stop and build another brig. Finally, on August 26, the banks of the river widened giving way to the Atlantic. Sailing Northwards by intuition, as they had no charts, the Spaniards soon arrived at the coast of Venezuela. They had traveled for eight months since they left the Andes. The most powerful river on earth had finally been discovered.

EVERYBODY'S AND NOBODY'S LAND

News of the Spanish discovery soon found its way to explorers of several European nations. The legend of the Amazons and of lands filled with riches soon attracted pirates and explorers, banked by their governments to roam the savage territories of the new continent. Yet while the western coast of South America allowed for easy mobility, the northern side presented an almost impassable wall of tropical jungle. Still, a trickle of English, French, Spanish and Portuguese explorers occasionally penetrated the great forest adding their accounts to the indissoluble mix of facts and legends that began to abound.

Following the tracks of the Conquistadors came Jesuit friars and Dominican priests, raising small missions on suitable bends in the rivers. More importantly, they began to study and collect ethnographic data of the local Indians and soon were fluent in their languages and well versed in their costumes. The Indians, however, resisted to the attempts of assimilation and conquest and many were the European men of God who along side their soldiering counterparts found their end among the twisted roots of the jungle floor, impaled by an Indian arrow or bludgeoned by a heavy wooded tacape.

THE JOURNEY OF PEDRO TEIXEIRA

For more than 100 years, Spain accumulated precious knowledge about the Amazon Jungle. In 1493, in order to appease Spaniards and Portuguese, excited by the prospect of economic conquest from their voyages to the New World, Pope Alexander VI decreed that a line of demarcation be extended some 563 kilometers West of the Azores and the Cape Verde archipelago. One year later, the reports of Portuguese navigators influenced a change in policy and a new treaty was proposed and signed by both parties, pushing the imaginary line that divided the two countries' areas of influence a further 2084 kilometers westwards. According to this treaty, signed by representatives of the two crowns at the Spanish city of Tordesillas, whose name it acquired, all lands discovered west of the line would belong to Spain while those discovered to the East would be Portuguese. On October 28, 1637, that would begin to change.

Concerned about the lack of information about the region and informed of the growing Spanish influence in the Continent, the Governor of Pará shrewdly used the arrival in Belém of a small group of Spanish priests who had escaped an attack to their mission on the upper Amazon. By helping them he would be able to learn more about the vast area to the west of the settlement. Vowing to return them to Quito, he organized an expedition to sail upriver from Belém to the Andean city. To lead it, he picked veteran Captain Pedro Teixeira, an experienced soldier who in his 68 years had managed, among other exploits, to defeat French, Dutch and Irish forces, driving them from Brazilian territory. He was to register everything of interest found along the way. To conduct Friar Domingo de Brieba and the six soldiers and six Indians

In 1637, Pedro Teixeira defined the territorial limits of the vast Amazon Jungle when he led an expedition from Belém to Quito in Ecuador. (Pages 22/23) From that moment on, the Portuguese built several forts that line Brazil's northern border to this day. Fort Príncipe da Beira depicted here still stands amidst the trees.

of his party back to Ecuador, the Portuguese authorities made available 47 canoes and an escort composed of some 70 troops, and almost 1.000 rowers enlisted from friendly tribes. On the twenty-eighth the expedition finally sailed towards the west, the high Andes as its final destination. If sailing downriver had been an enormous challenge to Orellana some 100 years earlier, the route upriver would certainly be an incomparable deed to undertake. Using sails to harness the wind and finding refuge against wind and rain in the islands that dot the rivers, Pedro Teixeira sailed with the proficiency so common to Portuguese sailors of his time. He personally handpicked moorings where hunting and fishing were easy. Several were the times, when the soldiers of

The 18ᵗʰ Century was marked by several scientific expeditions sponsored by the principal European nations. Among these was that of Alexander Von Humboldt, a German scientist. He came to the jungle to study the region's fauna and flora hoping to find resources of economic value. Thousands of specimens were taken to the Old World. For over two hundred years the Amazon has been studied in great detail.

the expedition had to confront savage tribes of the middle and lower Amazon. The better military organization of the Portuguese and Pedro Teixeira's diplomacy prevailed and most of the skirmishes were resolved with minor consequences. As they approached the Tefé River a mutiny was in the makings, the lack of results and boredom taking over. Luckily they came across the Curuziari Indians whose custom it was to adorn their faces with small plates made of solid gold. In no time, the expedition had received an injection of enthusiasm and after trading with the tribe they were ready to resume their journey in search of further treasure. Several miles upriver the Portuguese encountered the bizarre Omaguá Indians whose exotic features inspired legends and lore which had terrorized European explorers for many decades. Close to the Andean foothills they entered Encabelado Indian territory. These were the same savages that had massacred the Franciscan mission to which Friar Brieba and his men belonged. As a precaution, Teixeira left a detachment of Portuguese troops ordering them to lift a palisade to defend themselves from possible attacks. That was the first of several Portuguese fortifications that would soon defend strategic bends in the rivers of the region and that would forever change the dominion of most of the Amazon. At the head of an advanced party composed of a few of his men, Pedro Teixeira continued towards the Andes, hacking away at the jungle for over 200 days. The small and flexible group finally reached the snows of the volcano Cayembe

from where the city of Quito could be reached in a matter of days.

It was under popular acclaim that the Portuguese entered the Andean capital, and after a brief rest they heard the news that the Viceroy of Peru had ordered that all help be granted to them for their return trip to Belém. He also determined that two representatives of the crown of Castile accompany the expedition in order to gain as much information as they could both from the journey westwards as well as from the return trip. One of the men chosen was Father Cristobal de Acuña a Jesuit who had just arrived from Spain to form a school at Cuenca, not far from Quito. On February 16, 1639, the Portuguese expedition finally left Quito for Belém trudging on the snows down into the jungle until they reached the rivers, which would carry them home. Six months were necessary for them to reach the palisade in Encabelado territory. Upon his arrival, Pedro Teixeira announced the orders he had received from the Governor of Pará upon leaving Belém and which determined that all lands and rivers found on the trip should be taken in the name of the Portuguese Crown. The result of this action pushed the Line of Tordesillas over 3.000 kilometers to the West defining Portuguese control over most of the Amazon. Throughout the years Portuguese forts consolidated the dominion of the vast jungle region. This situation would remain unchanged with Brazil's independence almost 200 years later. The trip downriver was undertaken in less than 120 days, quite a difference from the ten months of the western leg. In December 1639 the people of Belém once again lined the streets of the town to hail their men back. Two years had elapsed since they had left. As soon as he arrived in Belém, father Acuña, following instructions, boarded the first ship to Spain. He carried with him his precious notes, which would be published two years later bearing the title: *The New Discoveries of the Great Amazon River*. In his writings Acuña continues to fuel the myth of the Amazon Warriors and of the legends believed by Teixeira's men. These stressed the fears of the upper Solimões which included the existence of giants standing over three meters tall and of men with feet turned backwards as to allow them to leave footsteps which led their followers on the opposite direction which they had taken. It also describes the existence of a large number of animals, minerals and plants whose characteristics would bring great riches to those who sought them. The costumes of the local Indians, their medicinal plants, their tools, their techniques for hunting and fishing and their social behavior were published for the first time. The Spanish Priest observed the existence of cocoa, of the several types of timber found in the forest, of tobacco and sugar cane, of cotton, several saps, poisons, resins and oils which if combined with techniques in use by European society would have great use. Acuña's manuscript described the banks of the Amazon as a paradisiacal place, a narrative which if unable to boost Spain into conquering the vast territory, helped solidify an image that the passage of time was never able to dissipate.

The Scientific Journeys

If the first two hundred years of European presence in the Amazon were dedicated to the conquest of land and riches, the 18th Century saw the arrival of scientists devoted to the collection of the vast biological universe hidden in the rainforest. Intrigued by the exuberant nature and the proficiency of the local inhabitants in extracting food and medicines from the jungle, they began two hundred years of scientific exploration of the region's plants and animals.

In 1745, Charles Marie de La Condamine arrived in the Amazon to decide an important scientific discussion whose objective it was to determine whether the Earth was curved around the Equator and flat at the poles or if the opposite held true. With several prominent French scientists he left on a trip from Belém to Quito with the objective of measuring the exact length of a degree of longitude at the Equator. Once he had concluded his experiments, La Condamine decided to remain in the region to perform studies that ranged from botany and zoology to the ethnography of the local Indians. The 18th Century expanded the curiosity of mankind. Led by the new sciences, which were organized in method, researchers began cataloguing and ordering everything that existed on the Planet. The Amazon for these men became a huge and exuberant study area. Alexander Von Humboldt, Henry Walter Bates, Alfred Russell Wallace, Karl Friedrich Von Martius and several others took detailed studies about the region to their countries. The expeditions multiplied throughout the years, new knowledge stimulating further expeditions to explore the rainforest. Important scientific discoveries asked for further research which in turn led to further discoveries. Henry Walter Bates spent eleven years in the Amazon on behalf of the British Museum. When he returned he had collected 14.712 species which he took back to England. Alcide D'Orbigny traveled for hundreds of miles throughout the region before returning to Paris with over 10.000 plants

The Rubber Rush of the late 19th Century brought great prosperity to the Amazon. It was short lived however, as seeds were smuggled out to England and planted at London's Kew Botanic Gardens. Soon after they were planted commercially in Malaysia, Indonesia and Ceylon where better planning allowed for greater productivity thus dramatically lowering the price of rubber around the World.

and animals, many of which would form the base of important scientific research, which helped advance European industry.

Among de La Condamine's writings read before the Academy of Sciences in Paris, was a description of a tree called Heve by the natives, in fact the rubber tree which the local tribes used to make syringes with which they injected narcotic substances into their nostrils during festive occasions. The Portuguese in Pará had already learned with the Indians how to use latex to make boots and tarpaulins and how to make holes in the hulls of their boats impermeable. In 1839, Charles Goodyear invented the process of vulcanization, which would eventually allow the manufacturing of automobile tires. These were developed 51 years later by an Irishman named John Boyd Dunlop. Four years later Edouard Michelin built the first interchangeable tire. Suddenly the Amazon became the focal point of a great rush. But instead of gold, it was rubber that the adventurers sought. The region prospered like never before. Manaus flourished as the Rubber Capital of the World attracting the most modern and luxurious goods from Europe to satisfy the veritable swarm of merchants who made its muddy riverbanks their home.

Early in the 20th Century, almost 40% of Brazil's foreign debt were paid solely by taxes charged for the extraction and export of rubber. Manaus traded directly with Europe and North America, as roads and railroads linking it to Brazil's major population centers were nonexistent. However, around 1910, seeds smuggled out of the country in an Englishman's hollow cane were planted commercially in Malaysia, Indonesia and Ceylon. Soon rubber prices plunged and the Amazon returned to its pitiful reality.

The History of the Amazon in the almost 500 years since it was first seen by European eyes is a succession of expeditions and conquests, both military and scientific. Men of the most diverse nationalities wandered through the jungle, sailed down the wide rivers, sweated in the dense humidity in search of gold, spices, myths and legends, plants and insects, saps and minerals and medicines. Spaniards, Portuguese, Englishmen and Irishmen, Frenchmen and Germans, Russians and Ameri-

Aerial view of the town of Porto Velho, capital of Rondônia taken in 1910. Built on the banks of the Madeira River, it was born as a trading post. Today it is a modern city with road links to Brazil's southeastern region.

In the early 20th Century major industrial projects were built in the Amazon in an attempt to tap the gigantic resources of the jungle. Most, like the Madeira-Mamoré railroad, which was built to carry rubber to the Atlantic Ocean by means of the Amazon River, ended in failure. During the lying of the tracks over 6.000 workers were killed, mostly by disease.

cans all determined the History of the great forest throughout the years. The people who were conspicuously absent in the great conquest, however, were exactly those through whose territory the great rivers ran, and on whose soil the roots of the giant trees anchored their mighty weight. Absent from the great Amazonian adventure were those who needed it the most. The Brazilians.

SOME VERY SPECIAL MEN

Until the early 20th Century, Brazil was no more than a narrow strip of land developed along the coast after several years of maritime commerce made easy by the country's long Atlantic littoral. The hinterland was dotted with a few scattered villages, desolate towns and a few farms occupied by the same families for Centuries.

There was practically no link between the coast and the interior except perhaps in the Southeast, the country's richest region which concentrates the states of Rio de Janeiro, São Paulo and Minas Gerais, the most populated and progressive. Between the Southeast and the Northeast of the country there were no roads or highways, all transportation being made by boat either along the coast or down the smooth flowing São Francisco. The Amazon and a good portion of the Central Highlands were left untouched for four centuries, their economies fending for themselves.

It was in the early days of the 20th Century that a young Brazilian Army officer drove into the vast interior capturing the imagination of a good portion of the population for the need to integrate Brazil's wilderness. Cândido Mariano da Silva Rondon was born in 1865 in Mato Grosso, a descendent of Bororó, Terena and Guamá Indians. He enrolled in the Army and in 1890 he graduated as a military engineer. As a Captain he took part in the expedition tasked with the lying of telegraph lines which would link vast portions of the interior to the cities of the coast. He also took part in the construction of the railroad that ran from Cuiabá to the Araguaia River. Throughout his career Rondon was always drawn to the interior. As a Major, he lay some 18.000 kilometers of telegraph lines as well as 17 transmitting stations in the Central Highlands, while as a Colonel he took the telegraph to the Amazon establishing lines for another 1.400 kilometers in the bush. He was instrumental in raising the topographical features of several portions of Goiás, Mato Grosso and the then unmapped Amazon Region. And in 1910, already a General, he became President of the Indian Protection Service inaugurating the Brazilian style of caring for its indigenous populations. According to Rondon's humanistic approach, it was paramount that when dealing with the Indians, one was to *die if necessary; but never to kill...*. Thus Brazil inaugurated a unique

No Brazilian inspired his countrymen as much as Marshal Cândido Mariano da Silva Rondon (standing third from the right). A defender of the Indians he was the father of Brazil's respect for its indigenous cultures. His several expeditions to the vast hinterland inspired the Brazilian Army's young Officer Corps to pioneer the country's interior.

manner of protecting its Indians, a practice which allowed it to arrive at the threshold of the 21st Century with one of the World's largest indigenous populations, in contrast to other societies where primitive peoples were decimated by more violent development.

Throughout the vast interior, Rondon's expeditions left behind settlements and villages, collected huge knowledge about the ways of the backcountry and welcomed Indians to their ranks. In all of his journeys he brought to the wilderness the comforts of progress and the presence of the Brazilian Government. Facing disease, torrential rains, the discomfort of life on the outback and the dangers of being attacked by savage Indians or wild animals, Rondon never relinquished his mission of developing the long forgotten interior. Yet, perhaps even more important than the deeds of the man himself, was his capacity to inspire a whole generation of young Army officers who turned their eyes westwards. Young men who, at the controls of flimsy aircraft of canvas and wood would finally turn the dreams of Centuries into reality.

INTERMINABLE RICHES
TAPPING THE RAINFOREST

The North of the South American continent is covered by a vast forest. Extending for over 6.5 million square kilometers, the Amazon is one of the most unknown and mysterious places on Earth. Its landmass amounts to an area equivalent to one third of the surface of the continent, occupying large portions of the territory of nine countries: Peru, Colombia, Venezuela, Ecuador, Bolivia, Guyana, Surinam and France, represented by its overseas territory of French Guyana. And yet, it is in Brazil that most of the forest which is attracting the attention of the globalized world is located. Some 85% of the jungle is in Brazilian territory making up almost 61% of the country's landmass. Brazil encompasses 5,08 million square kilometers of tropical forest, although only 16,5 million of its people, or 12% of the total population make the Amazon their home. In the nine Amazonian states – Acre, Amapá, Amazonas, Maranhão, Mato Grosso, Pará, Rondônia, Roraima and Tocantins – people live in what is one of the less densely populated areas on the planet. There are only 3,2 people per square kilo-

meter, a very scarce number, especially if compared to other areas of the Globe such as Japan (332/km^2), England (239/km^2), Germany (229/km^2), Italy (190/km^2), France (105/km^2) and even countries with larger areas such as the United States (29/km^2) and Brazil (which in great part due to the Amazon amasses only 19 inhabitants per square kilometer.

Perhaps what is most impressive about the Amazon is the giant size of the forest – which when flown over, extends itself as far as the eye can see. Most of it with no place to land. And covered by dense foliage, which suffocates the senses when penetrated. The endless proportions of its great distances are also amazing. To understand its extension it suffices to examine the distance by riverboat between Belém in Pará and the western city of Cruzeiro do Sul in Acre, a trip equal in size to that extending from Recife on Brazil's northeast coast to London, England.

The Amazon is nine times the size of France, and fourteen and a half times the size of Germany. Fifty five percent as large as the United States, and even Argentina, the World's eight largest nation would fit one and a half times in it.

This huge hot and humid region, where the trees grow over ground composed of decomposing leaves shelters vast riches under the vast forest canopy. In fact, the very future of the Planet will depend upon

Few are the regions of the Planet, which offer as many unexplored resources as the Amazon. In days when most countries are fully exploiting their natural resources, the Amazon is a beckoning expanse dominated by nature. (Pages 32/33) Bauxite is extracted from a mine at Porto Trombetas, in northern Pará. Among the several minerals that abound in the Amazon are cassiterite, gold, manganese, huge deposits of iron ore and niobium, a strategic mineral that is important in the computer and aerospace industries.

it if the rampant destruction of the atmosphere, a by-product of the fierce pollution brought about by the enormous output of the great industrial nations of the northern hemisphere continues.

Of these riches, by far the most important runs in the vast river basin that flows from the Andes to the sea and which make Brazil the second largest fresh water reservoir on the Planet, the first being the polar caps. Rivers run along an area 4,8 km² wide dumping some 20% of all the fresh water that flows into the oceans. To have a better picture of what this means, it suffices to compare the flow of the basin's largest river, the Amazon to that of Great Britain's most celebrated river. All the water that the Thames takes to the sea in a year equals the volume of water deposited by the Amazon in the Atlantic on a single day. According to the United Nations, the population of the Planet will grow from the current 6 billion people to 9,4 billion by 2050. The organization's scientists, predict that on that year some 42% of the World's population will suffer from lack of water, either in a state of insufficiency, a situation characterized by the availability of less than 17.000 m³ of water per person, per year (24% of the population) or in a state of scarcity (18%) with less than 1.000 m³ per person. As populations continue to grow, water will, without a doubt, be the Planet's most precious commodity.

Besides fresh water, the Amazon's myriad rivers offer endless sources of hydroelectric energy and huge potential for fisheries capable of feeding a large portion of Brazil's population. Other raw materials hidden under the jungle canopy are capable, if explored, to bring much needed economic growth not only to the region but to the entire country, a nation much in need of resources to bolster its ailing economy.

Giant deposits of minerals including iron ore, bauxite, cassiterite, gold, manganese, and titanium can be found in odd spots throughout the forest. Huge uranium reserves, capable of supplying years of energetic output for Brazilian homes and industries are also known, while many others lie awaiting discovery. In the state of Roraima alone, there are vast deposits of niobium, a strategic mineral considered the steel of the 21st Century, and which is strategic for the computer and aerospace industries. The Amazon holds over US$ 1.6 trillion in known mineral deposits alone as well as considerable oil reserves particularly in the Javari River region along the Peruvian border. Located in an area of difficult access due to the large distances and impenetrable jungle, these deposits interest those who know the true extent of the Middle Eastern reserves, located in the easily accessible desert sands.

Plants also bring economic potential to the Amazon region. One third of the World's tropical forests are located within the area encompassed by the vast basin. Over 300 million hectares of dense forest and 140 of more accessible open jungle comprise an amazing variety of plant species. In noble woods alone, the types preferred by the industrialized markets, reserves reach an estimated 45 billion cubic meters, or the equivalent to US$ 1,7 trillion. This amount would be easily capable of settling the country's foreign debt more than eight and a half times. Sold by several Indian tribes at an average

A centuries old Brazil Nut tree reaches for the skies in Breves, Pará. Exported in large quantities, mostly to the industrialized European, North American and Asiatic markets, the noble woods of the Amazon are extremely valued. An effective campaign must explain the results of this commerce in order to decrease the excessive deforestation brought to the region. (Pages 36/37) In the depths of the jungle, near the western locality of Cruzeiro do Sul, a Katukina Indian gathers leaves used as an antidote for the rattlesnake bite. Researchers living for years with the local Indians study their thousand-year-old medicines in order to have their formulas synthesized in laboratories for commercial sales.

US$ 16,00 per log, jacaranda or mahogany reach market prices of US$ 1,600.00 in the world market. It is therefore not surprising that portions of the jungle are brought down at the rate of 2.5 million hectares a year, having reached a total of 41.5 million hectares of the entire rainforest.

This indiscriminate deforestation, besides providing the markets of the northern hemisphere with cheap high quality woods, allows farmers to prepare grazing land for cattle which is timidly beginning to find its way into the dry areas of the Amazon. The jungle however, holds riches worth more than the economics of cattle. The Amazon has the largest deposits of biological material on the Planet, a resource which is gaining importance as genetic engineering develops and practically any cellular component found in nature is being duplicated in the laboratory, a technique which promises to revolutionize medical science. Each hectare of Amazon jungle possesses some 200 different species of trees, its rivers 1,400 types of fish and the forest canopy over 1,300 different birds as well as an incalculable number of reptiles and insects. Scientists believe that there are over two million different species of animals in the Amazon jungle. Some 22% of all known plants also originate from the forest, a total of almost 56,000 different species. To understand these numbers it should suffice to say that some 2,500 different types of trees grow in the Amazon while in France there are no more than 50 different species. The Amazonian trees offer a vast variety of seeds, fruits, fungi, saps, roots and bacteria, each possessing an intricate biological code ready to be deciphered by scientists working for the World's great industrial conglomerates as well as for the governments of richer nations. Today, the Amazon is by far the most important source of pharmaceutical and biochemical products in the Planet. These resources are readily exported from the jungle only to return to the market in the form of expensive medicines which most of Brazil's population is unable to purchase, let alone know that they originated from their country's territory. Protected by complex and well-structured patent laws, these products are able to hold their market shares against all forms of local competition. While the region's inhabitants sustain themselves with the rubber, guaraná, timber, Brazil Nut, piaçava and jute fiber industries, researchers, many times posing as tourists indulge in a veritable rush for medicinal, aromatic, toxic, oil-rich, fibrous and protein-rich plants. For beetles, larvae, frogs, snakes, fish, bats, tree barks, orchids and other parasites, as well as herbs and other products which are used as drugs for the pharmaceutical, textile and cosmetic industries. They are also used as insecticides, fixers and herbs for phytoterapical products as well as for use by government security agencies as poisons, serums and narcotics. In no other region of the Planet are there as many natural oils as in the Amazon. Over 600 plants produce oils such as the babaçu, the andiroba and the copaíba among several others. More than 40% of the prime-resources for the pharmaceutical industry come from plants, some 25.000 different types being used to produce medicines. How many of these come from the Amazon is yet to be determined. What is known, however, is that some 25% of all of the medicines produced worldwide stems from the South-American jungle.

A German researcher hired by the New York Botanical Gardens shows a specimen that composes the herbarium at UFAC – Acre State University. Several scientific cooperation programs coordinated by the Brazilian Government demonstrate that joint studies conducted for the benefit of mankind can be organized by Brazilian institutions with successful results.

But how do the researchers discover these tropical components? With the help of anthropologists and biologists working deep within the jungle – sometimes living among the local tribes or with the inhabitants of the river banks – they learn how primitive medications and infusions used to cure diseases of various types are prepared. Once identified, these components are extracted from the forest and analyzed to determine what the active elements – with anaesthetic, analgesic, scarring or other therapeutical factors are. After being tested, their active principals are isolated and fractionated to determine if they can be duplicated in laboratory in an economically viable manner, or if is better to explore them directly from nature. Once that decision is made, the company begins production and commercialization on a worldwide scale, including the region from where the end product's prime resources were extracted. Once patented these formulas gain international protection even from those who have been using the medicine in its natural form for generations. DNA banks are fed with all of these substances and even with blood cells, in order to provide a general picture of the Amazon's genetic universe.

Possessing over 30% of the Earth's biodiversity, the Amazon region is a veritable treasure chest of genetic materiel, which will undoubtedly bring great benefit to future generations. In tapping this biological wealth Brazil expects to understand the intricate genetic world available in its largest unexplored region.

And it is not only for scientific studies that plants and animals are extracted from the Amazon jungle. The illegal commerce of exotic plants and animals attracts an ever-growing number of traders to the rainforest, avid to export beautiful specimens that are often ill equipped for life in colder climes. Colorful birds, tropical fish, exotic reptiles and mammals are all smuggled from the region to feed the growing demand from common people in the richer nations, interested in having a small portion of the Amazon forest in their living rooms. Unaware that they are fomenting the gradual destruction of the Rainforest they pay exorbitant prices for specimens that are rapidly beginning to disappear from the jungle.

This silent commerce – which occurs daily amidst the trees, and whose gigantic proportions remain unknown to the Brazilian population – haven't been curbed in an effective way by the local authorities who are mostly involved with other problems of larger and more urgent proportions.

One of these is the growth of drug trafficking. When hunted down by the authorities of their native countries, namely Colombia, Peru and Bolivia, members of major drug cartels have been migrating across the border into the Brazilian Amazon to plant Marijuana and its Amazonian variant, Epadu and to process Coca paste into Cocaine for export to the major consumer markets. What attracts these criminals to the Amazon are the large expanses of virgin territory. The rivers and airspace over the jungle have always allowed a comfortable transit of contraband in a region that has remained in its natural state for centuries.

Besides the traffickers and smugglers for whom the borders are mere lines on a map, the Brazilian authorities have been monitoring for decades the actions of guerrilla groups from neighboring countries that insist on finding refuge on this side of the border every time the local armed forces plan an offensive. On the hot pursuit, they sometimes cross the border themselves creating a situation that is considered unacceptable by the Brazilian Government, whose policy has always been to maintain a respectable distance from its neighbors' internal problems.

And in the midst of all these problems lie the indigenous populations, who are unwillingly brought into the center stage of Amazon politics. Brazil is home to a little more than 200,000 Indians, an equivalent of 0.13% of the national population. The Government has set aside a total of 988,062 km² as Indian land where the tribes are protected and capable of developing their commerce and traditions. These reserves are the equivalent to some 11.56% of the entire Brazilian territory, a number that alone shows the deep concern of the country's government with its native populations. There are 133,600 known Indians in the Amazon and they hold over 1,040,000 km² of the forest. Therefore 0.8% of the population owns 20% of the land. The state of Roraima, rich in strategic minerals for the computer as well as aerospace industries has the largest proportion of Indian land. Over 57,27% of its territory belong to several tribes. The FUNAI – which is the Government branch that oversees all indian activities has been undertaking a project to guarantee the integrity and support to all of the tribes spread along the large basin. The existence of the Brazilian tribes has been the center of much discussion as pressure groups have been trying to characterize them as independent groups with ethnical and cultural differences to those of the Brazilian population. Among these tribes are the Yanomami of the Brazil/Venezuela border whose hamlets lie in niobium rich lands. These groups have searched for excesses and injustices against the Yanomami by Brazilian authorities but so far these searches have proved fruitless. On the contrary, the efforts of the Brazilian Government in defending their Indians' integrity have so far been a beacon in the way primitive peoples must be integrated to existing nations, a practice in which Brazil has unfortunately not had many examples to follow. Along with the myriad races that compose Brazil's ethnic buildup, the Indians have found sanctuary and appreciation among the country's large population.

Brazil's Amazon region, an area of great importance for the future of mankind has long been trespassed by industrial groups of many nations, most intent on developing vast tracts of jungle for their own benefit despite the harm their projects may bring to the rainforest. It has also been a haven for groups of international drug smugglers whose illicit activities bring harm to the World's economies and whose actions threaten the integrity of sovereign nations. Few are the nations in the World that still have to develop over half of their national territories, something which Brazil has been undertaking in a gradual and cumulative way. Throughout the years, the Nation's eyes have turned toward the Amazon. But not too long ago, the Government as an active and present entity dominated no more then a thin 200-kilometer strip along the coast. The vast interior had been left unsettled. In the early days of the 20th Century, the Brazilian hinterland was ready to be discovered.

(Pages 42/43) A merchant of medicinal herbs practically disappears inside her stand at the market in Manaus. From these leaves, seeds and roots the local population extracts medicines that cure different diseases such as kidney problems, allergies, dermatological diseases as well as several others. (Pages 46/47) Roads of Amazon life. The rivers of the Amazon provide not only abundant deposits of fresh water but food for the local population as well as their main transportation routes. As the population of the Planet grows, fresh water becomes an ever more important commodity. The rivers of the Amazon will soon become the producers of one of the most important resources in the planet, drinking water.

Amazônia Brasileira
Brazil's Amazon Region

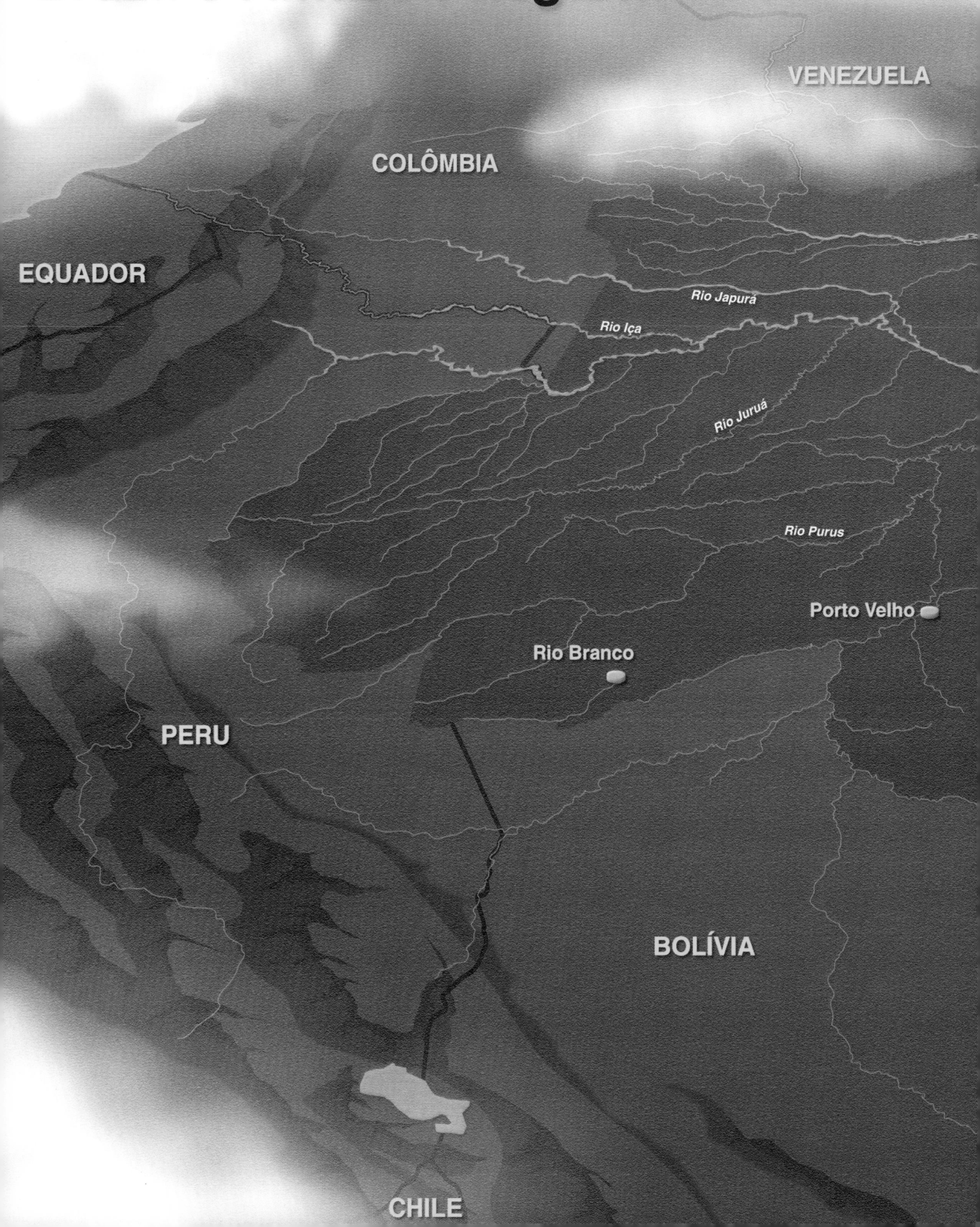

VENEZUELA

COLÔMBIA

EQUADOR

Rio Japurá

Rio Içá

Rio Juruá

Rio Purus

Porto Velho

Rio Branco

PERU

BOLÍVIA

CHILE

GUIANA
SURINAME
GUIANA FRANCESA
Boa Vista
Rio Branco
Macapá
Rio Negro
Rio Amazonas
Belém
Manaus
Santarém
Rio Xingu
Rio Solimões
Rio Tapajós
Rio Iriri
Rio Madeira
Rio Jamunxim
Rio São Manuel
BRASIL
Rio Jurema

TAKEOFF TOWARDS THE OUTBACK
BIRTH OF THE MILITARY POSTAL AIR SERVICE

Daybreak had come without the customary fog so typical of winter mornings. It was past one in the afternoon and the Curtiss Fledgling biplane with the prefix K-263 purred softly as it warmed its engine for takeoff from the grass strip at Rio de Janeiro's Campo dos Afonsos. In the open cockpits two young officers made the final checks and adjustments before committing themselves to flight. In front sat Lieutenant Casemiro Montenegro Filho, his white flight cap kept firmly in place by the goggles still affixed to his forehead. In the back seat Lieutenant Nelson Freire Lavénère Wanderley checked his maps for the umpteenth time, making sure the flight's route was correctly planned. Commander of the Training Flight of the Mixed Aviation Group of the Brazilian Army, Lieutenant Wanderley would be the navigator on the first leg of the mission for which the two flyers had been preparing since May. Lying at the floor of the cockpit was a postal bag, which was to be delivered at the main office of the Postal Services in São Paulo, 370 kilometers away. What is today a small distance demanded precise training in those days. The Fledgling carried a removable petrol tank above the wing and slightly ahead of the front cockpit. It was capable of extending the aircraft's range to almost 600 kilometers, more than enough to cover the necessary distance. Flying at 120 kilometers an hour, it should take the two men no more than three hours to reach São Paulo.

Suddenly the Curtiss Challenger's engine was revved to takeoff speed and the small square shaped biplane commonly known as Frankenstein* began its takeoff run and soon reached for the sky. It gained height circling slowly around the field and the nearby neighborhood of Realengo and was soon flying over the fields of Campo Grande. When they reached the Santa Cruz lowlands, the two flyers saw out in the distance, the deep blue sea separated from the muddy waters of Sepetiba Bay by the thin strip of sand that forms the Marambaia sand spit. Curving slightly to the right, Lieutenant Montenegro lined his fuselage to the long strip of sand, the aircraft's nose pointing to the hill that marks the westernmost limit of the long stretch of land that outlines the great Bay. Checking the instruments on the panel the two pilots soon realized that strong headwinds reduced their speed to 100 kilometers per hour. Immediately they gained altitude trying to reach 3.000 feet as early as possible in order to negotiate the most difficult obstacle of their trip. With the imposing Ilha Grande passing under the left wing, the two pilots looked in awe at the giant wall of rock and jungle that rose on their right hand side slowly surrounding them as they entered the depths of the Bay of Angra dos Reis. Over a hundred islands dotted the azure waters but the flyers had little time to admire them as they were now battling even stronger winds which further reduced the aircraft's speed to 90 kph. In this region the peaks

---

A WACO CPF-5 flies over the Paraíba do Sul River on a typical Airmail mission.

At the time aircraft cannibalization was a customary practice. Each operational aircraft was in fact a heap of parts taken from its pairs. Later, and because of its airmail flights the Curtiss Fledglings also became known as the Globetrotters.

rise to 1.500 meters and are covered by dense Atlantic jungle. There are no fields or roads to this day and the clouds often lie over the mountaintops reducing visibility at a rapid pace. The winds play games around the mountain peaks creating treacherous turbulences, which heightened by the thermals of the afternoon tossed the two Lieutenants around the sky. When they passed Parati they had reached their desired altitude and without a doubt looked down with a mixture of worry and enchantment at the thick jungle that slowly took the place of the placid waters of the Atlantic underneath the bouncing Fledgling. The loss of the engine there would certainly leave them in a very tough situation. The region over which they were flying is one in which the precarious nature of flight is more often remembered. Slowly, however, the towering walls of the Atlantic Range gave way to the green fields of the Paraíba River Valley, and with the sky rapidly taking on the pastels of dusk, the Army biplane with Lieutenant Montenegro navigating from the rear seat flew on towards São Paulo. The two anguished aviators prayed for speed as the rapid approach of night slowly began turning the distinctly marked ground into a black cloak of darkness. It was night when they finally saw the lights of the great city. In vain they tried to find the runway at Marte airfield but they

Nelson Freire Lavénère Wanderley was the navigator on the first flight...

knew that they would never find it in the dark. Suddenly the racetrack of the São Paulo Jockey Club at the Mooca appeared below K-263 and Montenegro lost no time. He found a long approach and in no time the two flyers felt the thin tires touching the grass of the racetrack, wet from the dew of the early evening. When the engine was finally switched off the two young officers looked at each other knowing that they still had a mission to fulfill. They grabbed the postal bag and left their plane behind to find their way to the offices of the postal service. The racetrack slept while the two Lieutenants climbed over the outer walls to hitch a ride with a passing motorist and a short while later were at their destiny where they delivered the postal bag and sent a mission accomplished message to their home base at Campo dos Afonsos. It was June 12, 1931 and the first line of the Military Postal Air Service had just been inaugurated. Brazil would never be the same again.

READY TO GROW

In the early days of the 20th Century, the Brazilian Armed Forces composed only of the Army and the Navy already looked at aviation with interest. The recent escapades of a fellow Brazilian on the Parisian fields of Bagatelle had captured, since 1906, the

50

imagination of an entire generation of youngsters. The flights of Santos-Dumont were also instrumental in France, whose aviation became the most advanced in the World. Beginning in 1910, Brazil began receiving the visit of several adventurers who would exhibit their aerial skills in return for a pre-established purse. A few years later, both the Army and the Navy sent young Lieutenants to flight schools in France. And in 1913 both forces chose students for the recently formed Brazilian Military Aviation School which due to the inexperience of the few instructors, of a handful of accidents and of the constant lack of supplies partially due to the outbreak of World War I, closed soon afterwards. The Navy then formed the Naval Aviation School at Galeão Point in the early days of 1916. Brazil's military aviation refused to die. With equipment from several sources and American instructors it soon graduated its first class. When Brazil declared war on the Central Powers the Navy sent a small group of aviators to England where they flew patrol missions with the Royal Naval Flying Corps. The Army also had its mind set on possessing its aviation branch and in 1918, a small French Military Mission arrived in Brazil to assemble the Military Aviation School at Campo dos Afonsos, a distant outskirt of Rio de Janeiro, then the country's Federal Capital. A year later the school was already in opera-

...Casemiro Montenegro was the pilot.

tion and twelve months later the first pilots were graduating. Operating with French built Nieuport, Spad, Caudron and Morane biplanes and adopting tactical doctrines originating from that country's operations in the Great War, the school soon became the focal point of Brazilian aviation. However the doctrine generated for the school kept the local pilots flying inside what was called "the Afonsos Cylinder" a cone shaped piece of sky with the school in the center. Its limits extended for no more than 10 kilometers around the field, any longer flights being frowned upon. The young pilots of the Brazilian Army knew little more than the immediate fields around the school.

In the early twenties, French pilots brought three Breguet XIV aircraft to Brazil. Unloaded at Rio de Janeiro port and assembled at the Military Aviation School, the planes were destined to reconnoiter the route between Rio de Janeiro and Santiago in Chile by way of Buenos Aires in the south. And the route that linked the Brazilian capital to Natal in the country's northeast coast, the ideal place for a seaplane base to serve as the first replenishment spot on their way from Europe. Their objective was the opening of a postal air service system, which would be named Latécoere. In 1927 the company was sold to a rich French businessman residing in Brazil and who immediately renamed it Aéropostale. And hav-

ing built landing fields at Rio Grande, Florianópolis, Santos, Vitória, Caravelas, Salvador, Recife and Natal it gained a support network along the Brazilian coast and was soon profiting from the transport of mail and newspapers. Each time they stopped at Campo dos Afonsos, the French pilots left their Brazilian Army counterparts awestruck with the stories of their adventures in the skies above the South American continent while the latter wished that someday, they too, would be able to break the imaginary barrier that kept them close to the school. Despite the fact that the Aéropostale flights were limited to the coastline, the young Brazilian flyers dreamed of using their aircraft to penetrate the country's vast outback taking civilization to the forgotten regions of the interior. The country was in the middle of a cultural revolution which centered on the famous "modern art week of 1922" in which the arts, the social sciences and political thought were exposed to radical new concepts. The 1922 and 1924 revolutions showed a desire to change Brazilian society, leading to the Revolution of 1930 when the country's political scene was radically transformed. The Brazilian Navy had been flying Fleet Airmail missions along the coast, taking important documents between shore based organizations and to ships on maneuvers at sea. It was therefore not surprising that young Army officers wanted their own Postal Air Service. In 1928, the new Army Aviation Arm formed its first class. Looking at their perennial condition as military aviators, the young flyers began questioning their function within the force. Among the several intellectual manifestations that reflected the desires of the new class of officer was an article published by Major Ajalmar Vieira Mascarenhas in a magazine called *National Defense*. The story bore the title *Towards Brazil, Away from Campo dos Afonsos* which was the motto of the young Army aviators who wanted to emulate their Aéropostale and Navy brothers and fly throughout Brazil, and who dreamed of changing the reality of their country's forgotten hinterland with their own young hands.

In 1931, an incident of great proportions would provide the conditions for a new mentality at Campo dos Afonsos. An Italian Count and his mechanic had taken off from São Paulo towards Campo Grande in the State of Mato Grosso. Somehow they had not arrived, causing great consternation. The Italian Government contacted the Brazilian authorities for help and despite never having operated outside the famous "cone" around Afonsos Field, two Army Potez-25TOE aircraft took off towards the interior of São Paulo State in search of the Italian plane. After a long search over the western edge of the state, one of the biplanes, flown by Lieutenants Francisco de Assis Corrêa de Mello and Nelson Freire Lavénère Wanderley finally came across the wreckage of the Italian aircraft over thick bush. Shortly thereafter the Count was rescued and was soon in good health. There were no doubts that Brazil's aviators could not only fly beyond the limits imposed on them but that their operations would bring great benefits to the nation. Shortly afterwards, in June 1931, War Minister, General José Fernandes Leite de Castro created the Military Postal Air Service. "*I felt it was important to change the face of the armies.*" would say the General, upon recounting his participation in the creation of the Postal Air Service. "*Instead of allowing them to remain unproductive...instead of doing nothing, we will do what the country needs.*" And in that manner, a visionary General, gave birth to one of his Army's most important dreams turning the propellers of his airplanes, once and for all towards the giant Brazilian outback.

BIRTH OF THE MILITARY POSTAL AIR SERVICE

In May 1931 the Army created the Joint Aviation Group. It would be the first operational unit of the

(Pages 52/53) June 12, 1931. Montenegro and Wanderley take off from Afonsos Field towards São Paulo. The real Curtiss Fledgling K263 was olive drab but this painting of the historic flight depicts the frailty of the planes with which the CAM began operating. (Facing page) In 1932 the CAM started receiving WACO CSO aircraft with which it was able to increase the number of lines that flew to all corners of Brazil. The Navy created the Naval Airmail Service using the same planes with floats.

newly formed Aviation branch, despite the fact that it continued to operate from the Aviation School. Its commander was Major Eduardo Gomes, a respected officer who was already somewhat of a legend in the Army. A revolutionary in 1922 when he participated of the famous march of eighteen rebellious officers against the government troops on the Copacabana boardwalk in Rio, he rebelled once again in 1924 and after being freed was readmitted to the force. His dreams of a better Brazil were incorruptible. He embraced his new mission with his customary steadfastness and began transforming army aviation, and more precisely the Postal Air Service which he was about to head, into the major instrument which he would use to take progress and well being to the forgotten outback.

He immediately created a Training Flight within the Joint Group. For its commander he appointed Lieutenant Nelson Freire Lavénère Wanderley. The unit was located at the Captain Rubens hangar, a precarious wooden hamlet on the edge of the field. Seven Curtiss Fledgling biplanes arrived to equip the flight. Soon afterwards Wanderley and Montenegro would take off for the historic Rio-São Paulo flight on the K-263.

One day after they dropped the postal bag at the São Paulo Postal Service offices, Wanderley and Montenegro returned to Rio. This time the first sat in the front cockpit, and chose the Paraíba River Valley route instead of the sea. In three hours and twenty minutes they were home. Major Eduardo Gomes already knew what the next step would be for the Postal Air Service. He decided that all flights would be made on a weekly basis, and training an integral part of the crews day-to-day activities. The Military Postal Air Service had been officially created but its initial name was soon changed to CAM – Correio Aéreo Militar

or Military Airmail Service. Soon several flights had been completed on the initial route. It was time to move further inland. And the first line chosen would be an extension of the São Paulo line to Goiás. The only problem was that the railroad only ran to the city of Leopoldo Bulhões. From there onwards, the fields were an indistinguishable vastness with no landmarks to guide the pilots. From that city onward it was unknown territory. Lieutenant Montenegro was chosen to reconnoiter the route to Goiás by land. He reached Leopoldo Bulhões by train and from there he continued on foot, on horseback and using any other means of transport on which he could lay hands upon. Knowledgeable about the flight envelope of the planes he flew, he set about to prepare landing strips at the locations he found appropriate for regular landings. He became a sort of "itinerant salesman" convincing mayors and authorities of the villages he chose of the advantages of helping him build runways. He told them of the progress aviation would bring to their communities. Each spot was handpicked by Montenegro, a veritable expert on the then infant mode of transportation, which he had chosen for his career. In October 1931 Montenegro once again took off in a Fledgling with his companion of the first Postal Flight, Lieutenant Wanderley. This time Goiás was their destiny. They would fly over the route he had painstakingly prepared. A few minutes after taking off, however, they came upon heavy clouds on the Atlantic Mountain Range and had to force land on a field. Montenegro was hurt in the crash and the plane was damaged beyond repair. But the Airmail Service tried again a week later. This time Wanderley's companion would be Lieutenant Joelmir Campos de Araripe Macedo. After innumerable adventures flying Fledgling K-272 they finally reached Goiás taking the Service once and for all to the Brazilian outback.

After six months of operations, the CAM lines covered 1,731 kilometers. Thirty-seven pilots had been deemed operational. It was time for the next step.

As rotas do CAM
Routes of the Brazilian Military Air Postal Service
1932 - 1946

Ano Year	Extensão da linhas Extension of Lines	Quilômetros percorridos Kilometers Flown	Horas de vôo Flight Hours	Passageiros transportados Passengers Carried
1932	3.630 km	127.100	865:00	17
1933	3.630 km	251.505	1.776:00	58
1934	7.600 km	615.785	4.279:00	121
1935	10.280 km	925.020	5.717:17	403
1936	11.743 km	1.080.939	4.449:03	577
1937	13.878 km	1.316.340	8.193:00	1.016
1938	14.916 km	1.663.409	10.093:00	1.072
1939	19.709 km	1.835.703	10.759:05	542
1940	19.096 km	1.541.797	8.625:48	759
1941	18.168 km	2.174.489	12.652:45	450
1942	23.414 km	2.416.917	14.758:15	428
1943	22.580 km	2.692.537	13.262:20	400
1944	33.993 km	2.566.942	13.173:45	544
1945	31.183 km	3.432.325	18.475:30	253
1946	49.496 km	3.722.454	14.992:80	14.154

Ilustração: Alex Argozino

Yet if the early pioneers of the CAM had undoubtedly shown courage and daring, they would also demonstrate that they possessed prudence. The terrain, which took them towards Leopoldo Bulhões, permitted simple and precise navigation, as all that was necessary was to follow the railroad. The fields and pastures of Goiás on the other hand, were extremely difficult to navigate over, as there were few landmarks to follow. Someday, somebody would get lost. Wanderley then decided to send one of his Lieutenants, José Vicente de Faria Lima to Goiás in order to solve the problem. The young Army flyer left towards Goiás taking along a NCO as a trusted aide. The two men decided to build large wooden signs with the letter G painted in white and arrows showing the way to Goiás at the many crossroads on the way. With the help and authorization of mayors and clerics, the two men painted the names of the towns on the rooftops of railway stations and churches along their way so that their colleagues could spot them from the air. Soon, as the CAM began to grow, this practice was followed throughout the country.

THE LINES MULTIPLY

In 1932 Brazil was torn by a Revolution between the Federal Government and the State of São Paulo. It had little influence on the day to day activities of the CAM, but in one aspect it brought great changes. It was the arrival of a little red airplane used for combat but which found a new role with the return of peace. The WACO CSO was a twin seat biplane equipped with a 250hp Wright R-760E engine, capable of reaching speeds of 209 kph and a range of 868 km. Superior to the Curtiss Fledgling in every aspect, the WACOs soon superseded that aircraft in the Postal routes. Soon after the end of the Revolution the Army created the 1st Aviation Regiment, which was composed of a fighter and a bomber group. It also encompassed a training flight in which the WACO CSOs were grouped.

The CSOs multiplied the number of localities reached by the CAM. In 1932 it started flying to Mato Grosso and Curitiba, and before the year was over a line to Fortaleza following the São Francisco River had been established. Throughout the vast interior the little WACOs began taking letters, newspapers, medicines, and small parcels to people who until then could only communicate with the great coastal cities through river traders or adventurers who occasionally reached their distant hamlets. The Airmail Service planes brought doctors who saw entire towns and often transported sick or wounded inhabitants to cities better prepared to heal them. And the people began to call them "the little red ones", as did the pilots. And soon they were the link between two very different Brazils.

In 1934, the Navy inaugurated the Naval Postal Air Service. Equipped with amphibious and land-based WACO CSO and WACO CPF-5s as well as WACO CJC with enclosed cockpits, it extended its lines from Rio de Janeiro to Santa Vitória do Palmar in the country's extreme south, with several stops along the way. The Navy soon developed several trunk routes from which secondary lines reached smaller locations near the coast or the riverbanks. In a short time the Naval Postal Air Service reached twenty cities along the Brazilian coastline providing the fleet with an efficient way of transporting its mail. The next step was the building of landing strips at chosen spots along the route, allowing land-based planes to fly as effectively as the seaplanes. The Navy's airfields as well as its aircraft were equipped with radio sets which provided them with excellent control of Naval Postal Air Service operations.

Shortly thereafter the Army began receiving new aircraft still in the form of WACOs, only this time they were of the CTO variant with elliptical wings, which gave it a more critical flight profile. The new plane didn't take long to acquire a reputation as a dangerous aircraft particularly after a fatal accident occurred at Campo dos Afonsos. But not even the new plane could hold the CAM pilots whose goal was to integrate the vast interior. Other types of WACOs soon followed bringing more comfort to the pilots, as they possessed enclosed cockpits, which gave them better protection against the wind and the rain. In a country of nicknames the new planes were soon dubbed Cockpit WACOs losing their factory designations soon after they were disembarked at the Rio de Janeiro docks! The first 25 of these aircraft started arriving in 1934. Capable of transporting five passengers they had the same performance of their earlier pairs. The cabin, however, provided not only greater comfort but also a better environment to navigate in.

In 1935 the CAM had opened lines throughout most of the coast and to remote areas in the Central Highlands. It was time to dare further and find a way to the Amazon. The great adventure, which would be the opening of the Tocantins Line, was about to begin.

THE TOCANTINS LINE

The new lines were always opened in the way Lieutenant Montenegro did on his journey to Goiás. Before the flying began, a land expedition surveyed the route. To explore the arduous way to the Amazon the Army picked a young Captain by the name of Lysias Rodrigues. In August 1931 he left Campo dos Afonsos toward Belém in distant Pará. Two Pan-American Airways employees asked to go along in order to determine the cheapest route between Rio de Janeiro and Miami. On a winter morning, they left Rio by train to São Paulo. From there Lysias would take another three trains changing at Campinas, Araguari and Ipameri, the third location already in Goiás. There the railroad ended, so the travelers rented an old Chevrolet truck with which they drove to São João da Aliança, passing by Cristalina, Planaltina and Formosa in that giant inland state. After eight days on the road, Lysias had found five ideal spots for landing fields which he dutifully made sure would be built by the local authorities. Every day he moved further inland, living the same hardships as the simple people of the outback, savoring the exuberance of nature at that distant land, and confirming his conviction of the interminable barrier that air transport would shatter forever. When they arrived at the Veadeiros Plateau they traded their car for five horses and three mules with which they crossed the imposing obstacle. Throughout the way Lysias practiced what he knew of medicine, his pharmacy being used to heal the locals who rarely saw a doctor. Finally they arrived at Cavalcante where another field would certainly change that in the not too distant future. From there they went to Palmas in what today is Tocantins, crossing seldom-traveled fields. They arrived six days and five nights later, to see the welcome sight of the Tocantins River running next to the town. From the top of the church steeple, Lysias Rodrigues chose the spot where yet another landing field would be built. Two days later he left town on board a canoe towards Porto Nacional. When they moored at the first stop along the way, a village aptly named Peixe, they discovered that the spot for a landing strip had already been picked and that work to build it would commence soon. Word of his arrival and of his objectives had preceded him. The canoe was traded for a larger riverboat and three days later; the three men arrived at Porto Nacional. Thirty days had passed since they boarded a train in Rio, and nine airfields had been demarcated. Captain Rodrigues' mission was running smoothly. At Porto Nacional the trio traded vessels yet again, and headed North passing the locations of Pedro Afonso, Carolina and Boa Vista. At each new place, a new runway was planned. An oar driven canoe was their next means of transportation, their supplies following on mule back on the riverside. The next stop was Imperatriz in Pará where another field

The WACO EGC-7s, known as New Cockpits, arrived in 1938 bringing greater comfort to CAM pilots.

was to be built. Continuing northwards they finally reached the Amazon, the fields giving way to thick forest. The animals soon began to disappear inside the foliage. Soon Marabá appeared in front of their boat, and it didn't take long for Lysias to kneel at the foot of a large tree while examining a long field, which would soon see the aircraft of the CAM landing there. They continued downriver on a paddle wheeler until they finally reached their destination, Belém. They had left Rio de Janeiro 52 days earlier. Seventeen new airfields were already being built throughout the Brazilian outback. Soon the CAM would be able to fly there. Four years later, on the fourteenth of November, Major Lysias Rodrigues accompanied by Sergeant Soriano de Oliveira left Afonsos Field on WACO CSO C-35 towards Belém. What had taken 52 days by land was flown in three! Three thousand five hundred kilometers had been trekked from the Capital to Belém. The Airmail Service had finally reached the Amazon!

Lysias Rodrigues would fly two more missions on this route before it became a regular line in 1939.

THE BOW AND ARROW AVIATION COMES TO AN END

In 1955 the Army bought 30 WACO CPF-5 aircraft increasing the number of platforms available for the airmail mission. Painted red, like the other WACOs they helped consolidate the image of the Army's, and consequently the Government's presence every where they landed.

On January 23, the following year, the CAM opened its first international route to Asuncion, Paraguay. The CAM was expanding rapidly always supported by the untiring Eduardo Gomes who controlled every detail of the service, helping and supporting all the ideas that could benefit the impoverished populations of the most distant places. He went as far as to personally purchase books, notebooks, medicine and whatever he could send through his pilots to con-

tribute to the efforts being undertaken to diminish the suffering and isolation of fellow Brazilians that he did not known, and would never see.

By the end of the 1930s the Military Airmail Service was firmly consolidated. Few were the mayors who did not covet a landing strip to receive the Airmail planes, and soon new extensions were being added to each line.

In 1938, thirty enclosed cockpit WACO EGC-7s arrived at Afonsos. Another seven would be assembled at the school depot, three years later. Of modern design, faster and with greater range than the previous generations of aircraft from the same factory, they soon earned the moniker New Cockpit WACOs in reference to the earlier type which had its nickname changed to Old Cockpit WACO! The new plane brought modifications that pointed to the arrival of a new generation of aircraft. Hydraulic brakes, better flight control surfaces, electric starters, were just some of the modifications incorporated to the plane. Its Wright Whirlwind R-760-E2 radial engine possessed 100 hp over the Old Cockpit version, which made it fly some 100 kilometers further at a relatively greater speed. The new WACO was the first sign that the typically Brazilian Bow and Arrow Aviation, in which flying was rudimentary, navigation had to be precise, and knowledge of the terrain and its landmarks flawless, was coming to an end. It was a time when the Airmail took hope and the symbolic presence of the Brazilian Government to its most remote corners. By 1939 the CAM had carried over 65.000 kilos in parcels over lines stretching for more than 19.700 kilometers. It accomplished with flimsy planes, the integration of the Brazilian population and the promise of the country's sovereignty over its vast territory.

Beechcraft UC-43/GB-2 Travelers designated C-43s by the Brazilian Air Force were the transition aircraft between the CAM and the new National Airmail Service (CAN). Flown by the Navy since 1940 in the Naval Airmail Service in the D-17A version, this plane was known as Beech Mono by the Airmail pilots who raved about its speed, range and new equipment such as retractable landing gear and radio compass.

WINGS OVER THE RIVERS AND THE FOREST
THE BRAZILIAN AIR FORCE UNRAVELS THE AMAZON

In 1941 the Brazilian Army and Navy aviation branches were joined into a single force. The Government had created the Ministry of Aeronautics and along with it, a fighting arm, the Brazilian Air Force (FAB). It came to life with a new philosophy of Unified Air Power, in which both the civil and military sectors of aviation would be co-ordinated by the new ministry. All the pilots, support personnel, bases and equipment of both services were taken over by the new force. On February 20, the CAM was also amalgamated with the Naval Airmail Service. Ministerial Decree number 47 created the National Airmail Service – *Correio Aéreo Nacional,* CAN which would be subordinate to the newly formed Directorate of Air Routes, whose Commander was none other than General Eduardo Gomes.

At no moment, however, did the operations cease. The ideals that had brought about the two Airmail Services of the past continued as strong as ever. It is interesting to note that the first time the idea of a Ministry of Aeronautics was brought up, was in a magazine issue suggesting its creation written thirteen years earlier. The author of the article had been the untiring Casemiro Montenegro Filho.

In 1942, the CAN acquired its first aircraft, six Beechcraft GB-2 biplanes (FAB designation C-43).

Flying in the heat of a noonday sky two Catalinas rule the airwaves over the great forest. Commanded by the men who gave birth to the CAM in the 1930s, the Airmail Service in the Amazon was instrumental to ensure that Brazil reached its farthest corners in an age when the Northern Forest was as exotic to Brazilians as it was to foreigners.

These joined another three D-17As of four that had been bought by the Navy in 1940. The FAB would eventually operate 51 of these airplanes, which were known as the *Beech Mono*. With its elegant silver finish and advanced equipment, the new plane was enthusiastically received by the young Airmail pilots. Besides their ability to fly at higher speeds than their previous mounts – 341 km/h instead of the WACOs 273 km/h – the Beechcrafts had almost twice the range – 1,286 km against the 900 km of the WACO EGC-7. The new plane was also radio compass equipped and possessed retractable landing gears, which offered a much more comfortable flight without the drag induced by a fixed gear set-up.

In 1942, Brazil declared war on Germany, Italy and Japan entering the Second World War on the side of the Allies. That conflict would not paralyze the National Airmail Service. Despite the scarce means at its disposal brought about by wartime restrictions, it continued operating albeit at a slower pace. The years of flying throughout the vast Brazilian expanses to which an entire generation of pilots had been exposed, soon made themselves felt in wartime operations. The Brazilian Air Force was born in battle, and despite the fact that some of its pilots had seen combat during the several revolutions which wrought havoc to the nation in the thirties, most had only flown in Airmail missions. The lack of any type of air navigation system had forced our pilots to learn how to fly their own style of nap of the Earth, in which several dives below the clouds are made to keep the ground always in view. Any other altitude would end any attempt to navigate. This type of flying had been well assimilated by practically every Brazilian pilot and had become second nature in the fledgling air force. This skill explains why when the United States Government began sending a huge number of aircraft to Brazil as part of the Lend Lease Program, USAAF crews were rapidly replaced by FAB men. Several accidents had been occurring during the ferry flights that brought several types of aircraft to Brazil, particularly over the Amazon and the northeastern coast. The Brazilian Government took over the mission and several hundred aircraft were eventually ferried to Brazil with very few incidents and only one fatal accident. And even that one occurred because of loose cargo inside the cockpit at the time of landing. Among the aircraft sent to Brazil were trainers, bombers, fighters, transports, patrol aircraft and other types. The training that the Brazilian pilots underwent in the Airmail Service had been responsible for their proficiency in negotiating the treacherous airspace over the cloud covered skies, and the tough navigation over the awe inspiring uniform carpet of trees so particular to the Amazon. When in 1944, a group of 50 pilots and some 400 mechanics were sent to Panama to undergo combat training before flying operationally in Europe, the skills acquired in the Airmail Service once again came in handy. Few in the group had any notions about fighting in the air. Only a handful had ever fired their guns or dropped bombs in their careers. Few, however, had difficulty learning the rudiments of air combat. All were experienced flyers, used to *hug the ground,* as they would say, in order to navigate by rivers, jungles, fields and mountain ranges that were used as landmarks on the Airmail routes and that made flying over Brazil a very precise art form. Some of those

young Captains and Lieutenants had mustered over 2.000 flight hours a mark which made them experienced airmen when compared to most of their American colleagues, fresh out of flight school. In a short time they were ready for combat, which they faced with gallantry in the skies over Italy under the symbol of the 1st Brazilian Fighter Group. The young Brazilian pilots possessed an uncanny experience in dead reckoning navigation and that allowed them in 1943 to open an extension of the Tocantins line to Cayenne in French Guyana with stops at Macapá and Oyapoc. Flying daily, the Airmail Service helped breach the distance between the cities of the southeast and the northeastern coast, a route in which roads and rail links were nonexistent. Passengers could only reach those parts of Brazil by ship or by airplane.

Despite its hardships, the Second World War brought great benefits to the CAN. Brazil held a strategic position in the South Atlantic. In the early stages of the War, Brazil presented an open flank on the Allied side for German invasion from North Africa. Its capture could threaten the southeastern United States. Later in the conflict the country's northeastern coast became the *Springboard for Victory,* allowing the reinforcement of North Africa by Allied planes in a gigantic air bridge to the captured territories of Algeria, Tunisia and Morocco. A large number of air and naval bases were built by the United States on the Brazilian coast, and soon an advanced network of runways and air navigation equipment to control the hundreds of flights that operated daily over the region was in place. Commanding the Second Air Zone was General Eduardo Gomes. Understanding the importance of

The Noorduyn Norseman exemplifies the ideal aircraft for the Brazilian hinterland in the early days of the Airmail Service. It had to land on short spaces, provide great range, and possess a rugged build and a cost-effective operation. This plane was extensively used by the Central Brazil Foundation.

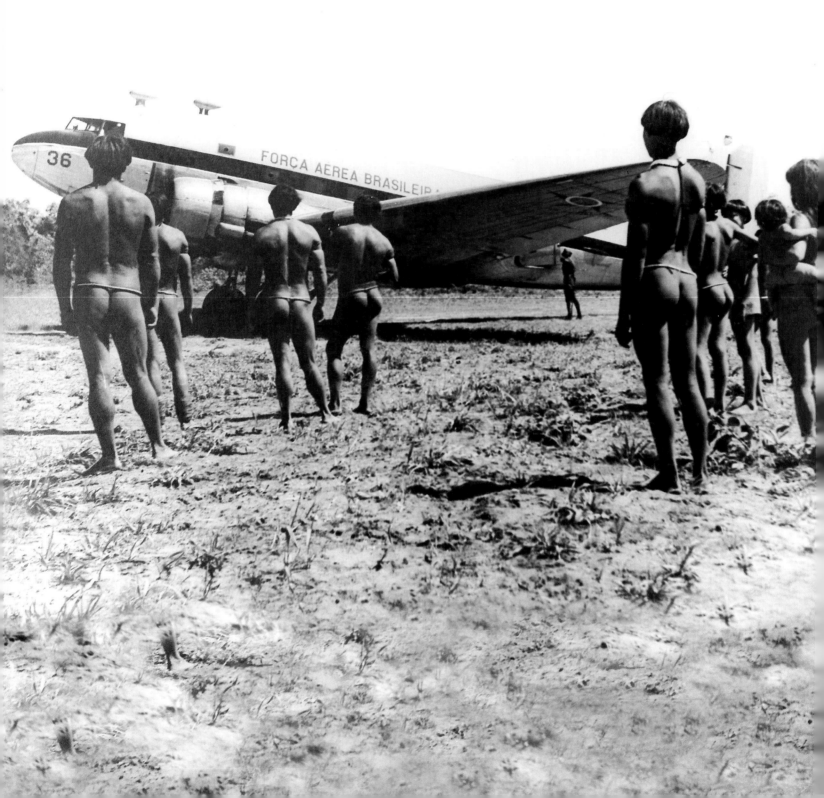

the National Airmail Service to the future development and integration of the country, he gave total support to the construction of those bases, knowing that they would become important staging areas for CAN planes as soon as the War ended. The massive presence of United States, as well as a few British and Canadian aircraft in Brazil's Northeast, demanded the use of modern air traffic control and air navigation equipment. Aircraft handed over to the Brazilian Air Force arrived with modern navigation equipment, enhancing the experience of the local pilots in navigation and traffic control. That was the case of the almost 90 twin engined Beechcraft planes, soon known as *Beech-bi* that slowly started to replace the *Little Red Ones* on the routes flown by the CAN.

The War in Brazil's Northeast was against German and Italian U-boats that swarmed the seas off the sun swept coast. Allied aircraft and surface forces combed the waters on search and destroy missions to clear the coast for convoys taking vital supplies to the war zone or to feed the US industrial war efforts. Making sure that the Brazilian Air Force was given growing responsibility in the combat operations, Eduardo Gomes and the American Command were able to implement the USBATU – United States Brazil Training Unit. This was a course with the objective of forming Brazilian aircrew in maritime patrol and anti-submarine warfare. The maritime patrol mission demanded precise navigational skills, as the flights were over huge expanses of water where there are no landmarks, navigation beacons or other equip-

The C-47 was the Brazilian Air Force's workhorse in its drive West. What U.S. Cavalry did for the development of the American West in the 19ᵗʰ Century, was replicated here by the Airmail Service one hundred years later. The young pilots saw their country with their own eyes learning that it was their responsibility to take the best the country had to offer to their isolated compatriots. Several Indian tribes made their first contact with the 20ᵗʰ Century through the wings of the Brazilian Air Force, their lives immediately improving in comfort and health.

ment capable of aiding the pilots. It was an operation that required acute situational awareness at all times. Thirty-six pilots and some 80 specialists graduated from the course forming the backbone of Brazil's patrol aviation branch. Most of them would fly Airmail missions once the war was over, and the experience gained over the sea would be passed along to the newer generations of CAN pilots.

The ferry flights from the United States to Brazil had exposed the FAB pilots to the modern air navigation equipment and state of the art techniques used by US air traffic control authorities. This contact, added to the operations with the USAAF in the Northeast, and to the joint training courses in Brazil and in American bases, provided experiences that were soon adopted by the growing Brazilian aviation. Airmail flights became safer due to the growing availability of air navigation equipment. Airports began receiving trained personnel, a flagrant difference from the old caretakers of olden days. Modern control towers, filled with adequate communication equipment sprang throughout the vast interior, and new aircraft allowed safer, more comfortable and efficient flights.

In 1944 the FAB began receiving C-47 aircraft, the famous Skytrains which were the virtual backbone of the Allied transport operations in all theatres during World War II. It brought great benefit not only to the Airmail Service but also to several Brazilian regions at the threshold of civilization. It also allowed the CAN to expand its lines internationally intensifying the country's relationships with several of its neighbors, previously separated by the huge distances or by the imposing natural barriers that are so common to South America. In May 1945, the Service began flying to Bolivia when Beech-bi 4203 arrived at Santa Cruz de la Sierra. The following year, on March 5, that line was extended to La Paz, a city whose airport lies at 4,000m. Douglas C-47 2016 was the aircraft responsible for opening that route. Flying over the Andes sometimes demanded climbing to 5,000 meters in order to rise above the weather. In these cases both the pilots and the passengers were forced to wear emergency oxygen masks. When reaching these altitudes the pilots would look continuously at their fingernails. If they turned purple, it was the first sign of anoxia, the dangerous narcosis caused by the lack of oxygen to the brain so common in those heights.

By the time the War ended, the Brazilian Air Force was able to purchase a large number of C-47s at very low price as the USAAF urgently needed to reduce its wartime numbers resorting to the sale of many of its assets which were deployed around the world. A total of 82 of these workhorses were used by the FAB during several years, the last being retired in 1983. Comfortable, capable of reaching great heights – 7,300ft – and equipped with powerful communications gear, their range reached 2,400 km at speeds of 300 km/h at 10,000 feet. However, it was its cargo capacity of around 1,500 kilos per plane that brought the greatest benefits to the Airmail Service. When it started flying with the CAN, the volume of supplies, equipment and passengers was multiplied tenfold allowing larger development projects to be carried out in more remote areas.

One of the lines opened with the C-47 reached the distant western border with Bolivia, a region hidden in the jungle and which was virtually unknown to most Brazilians. That line, to Acre, inaugurated in 1947 left Rio de Janeiro and reached Cruzeiro do Sul after thirteen stops along the way.

With the C-47 the CAN started to modify the country. It was therefore important that it grew in a solid, well-planned way, with well trained crews, well distributed supplies and a well-defined organization, capable of providing high levels of operational readiness. In the early days of the 1950s

the CAN was placed under the newly formed COMTA – *Comando de Transporte Aéreo*, Air Transport Command – that united all FAB transport assets under a central planning structure. In the 1950s it was not uncommon for the COMTA operations officer to have 25 or more aircraft on missions throughout Brazil or South America at any given moment. A line to Montevideo was established in 1956. In 1958 the CAN arrived at Quito. Even the United States was part of the CAN network, the Guyana line having been extended by way of the Caribbean Islands that same year. To provide a stop halfway between Rio and Manaus, the Air Force decided to build a field at Cachimbo, in the middle of the jungle. Major Haroldo Coimbra Velloso added his obstinacy to that of the Airmail pioneers and carved the runway into the heart of the forest. Facing tropical disease, the difficulty of transporting supplies to the region, and occasional attacks from the local Indians who used bows and arrows against incoming supply flights, the early pioneers of Cachimbo toiled against all odds to put a foothold in the jungle. A small dam and a power plant were built to supply autonomous electrical energy to the future base.

The Directorate of Air Routes, another of Eduardo Gomes' creations, followed the construction of new runways, inserting small detachments composed of two specialists with the mission of running and maintaining the beacons that served

---

When several of the pioneers of the CAM became Generals, they were able to continue the work they began when they were young. It was therefore not by accident that when Nelson Freire Lavénère Wanderley became Minister of Aeronautics, he authorized the purchase of C-130 Hercules aircraft, perhaps the most efficient planes ever flown by the Airmail Service. Capable of carrying a large payload for long distances, the Hercules is the backbone of the Brazilian Air Force's transport arm. (Pages 72/73) It was not only while airborne that the FAB developed the Amazon. In order to allow the operation of its aircraft amidst the dense jungle, the Air Force organized the COMARA – the Amazon Airport Commission. Toiling against the rugged forest, the constant threat of tropical disease, of poisonous animals and even of hostile tribes, the men from the COMARA never faltered, and at the end of their work had built a vast network of runways throughout the entire Brazilian Amazon.

the airfield, organizing landing and taxiing procedures, providing meteorological control and securing the communications with other fields.

In 1945, Casemiro Montenegro, then a Colonel embarked in a visionary project that would transform Brazilian aviation forever. Convinced that the level of technical education available in Brazil was below the standards observed elsewhere, and realizing that the country could build its own aircraft, he selected a huge tract of land in the region of São José dos Campos, in São Paulo state. It was a region located between the two largest Brazilian cities, easily reached both by road and railroad, supplied with ample electrical energy and with good climate. There, he built the ITA – *Instituto Tecnológico da Aeronáutica*, the Aeronautical Technical Institute – which later gave birth to the CTA – *Centro Tecnológico da Aeronáutica*, Aeronautical Technical Center – and later, in 1969, the Brazilian aircraft factory, Embraer. In 1954 the first class of Brazilian aeronautical engineers graduated at ITA.

Two years later, the Brazilian Air Force signed an important agreement with the SPVEA, a Brazilian Government development agency for the Amazon. Out of a total of seventeen airfields, there were only two paved runways throughout the entire region, in Belém and Manaus. The plan called

An Embraer EMB-110 Bandeirante, designated C-95B in FAB use, and belonging to the 7th Air Transport Squadron based at Manaus, overflies the Amazon River on a trip towards a jungle location. Designed to provide cargo and passenger transport to smaller locations, the Bandeirantes are among the most numerous aircraft in the Brazilian Air Force's order of battle. (Pages 76/77) The COMARA gets ready to hand over another runway. Few Brazilians are aware of the incredible work done by the Commission. Several localities in the forest needed runways but could not be reached by air. The men of the COMARA then acquired flatboats and began transporting the necessary materials and equipment on the river waters. To understand the size of their effort it suffices to remember the construction of the Tabatinga airport as well as the one in Vasquez Cobo, Colombia. Both were located in a region devoid of the rock necessary for their runways. Undaunted by the challenge, the COMARA flatboats took the crushed rock from the locality of Moura all the way to the two sites, over 2,100 kilometers away, a round trip that took over 40 days to complete.

for the construction of airfields in the most important cities of the Brazilian Amazon such as Macapá, Boa Vista, Porto Velho and Rio Branco. At strategic localities and at small intermediary destinations, runways were also to be built for use not only by the Air Force but also by the airlines that were expanding their operations to that part of Brazil. Little by little, the CAN brought its philosophy to the Amazon, safeguarding not only the region's defense but also its development. On December 12, 1956, decree number 40,551 created the COMARA, the Amazon Airport Commission.

The first Air Zone, whose area of responsibility embraced the Amazon, was commanded by Lieutenant Colonel João Camarão Teles Ribeiro, a man who understood the philosophy of the Postal Air Service and who was aware that the airplane was the only solution for the development of the Basin. His command would be a long one, extending until his promotion to Colonel and once again, upon his return as General and later as Major General. His long tenure in the Amazon allowed him to imbed the strong roots of the CAN's philosophy into every operational unit flying in the region. To head the COMARA he selected Major Protásio Lopes de Oliveira, a man as dedicated to the mission as he was. Together they created a well-oiled system to transport building material and equipment to the construction sites. Even tugboats and flatboats were organized into a flotilla owned by the Air Force to reach the places where aircraft could not go. A winning mentality that persists today was born in those early moments of the Amazon Airport Commission. Alongside the C-47, another airplane was instrumental for the growth of the CAN, particularly for a branch named CAN-AM, the Amazon Postal Air Service, also created in 1958. That plane was the Consolidated Vultee PBY-5/5A Catalina, both in its seaplane and amphibious versions. It had arrived in Brazil in 1943

and had been used during the War to patrol the South Atlantic. A shoulder winged amphibious twin engined craft; it was perfect for the Amazon. Several units were modified in the United States losing their armament and the observation windows, making them lighter and better capable of operating in the several rivers of the North. They were also fitted with troop seats, which allowed them to transport passengers. Their designation changed from the wartime PA-10 to the new CA-10 with which they would be used in their new mission.

Because of the lack of runways in the area for the C-47s, several remote corners of the Great Basin could only be reached with water landings. The local population tends to concentrate on the riverbanks and soon the big Cats were taking off from Belém Air Base to take solace and national presence to the Four Corners of the Amazon. From 1953 onwards, the PBYs began to fly on what became know as the Frontier Post missions on which they would land on rivers that ran alongside the Brazilian border replenishing the Army's frontier detachments which dotted the Solimões, Japurá, Içá and Negro rivers.

The CAN-AM ran along several lines that followed the vast river network where navigating was extremely difficult not only because of the lack of major landmarks, but due to the severe meteorological conditions that prevail there. These were known as the LIAs – Internal Amazon Lines and the LEAs, External Amazon Lines. The Solimões

Line followed the largest of the rivers to the western location of Tabatinga on the border with Peru and Colombia. The Negro Line reached distant Cucuí in the far northeast. The Javarí River Line extended to the west until it came to the villages of Estirão do Equador and Palmeiras do Javarí where Army detachments guard the border with Peru. The Purús and Juruá Lines, among others, took supplies to the riverine populations that crowded the river edge after the Catalinas flew scant feet above their villages to advise them of their arrival. At first there were 14 LIAs reaching 93 localities over 67,271 kilometers, which were flown by several aircraft on weekly, fortnightly and monthly frequencies. Other unplanned emergency sorties were also undertaken, mostly mercy flights, medevacs and humanitarian missions. To fulfill these missions the Catalina pilots were forced to land on rivers, which were not provided with proper markings or with canoes to help them reach the shore. This brought them great experience in jungle flying, and skills that would be useful in times of war. The CAN-AM missions were flown to guarantee the Brazilian Government's presence in the region as well as the maintenance of crew proficiency in the area. They also ensured the integration of the northern territory consolidating by air, the native and civilized populations of the Brazilian State. Medical and dental care was airlifted to where there was none, and schools were brought to the most remote areas in the wings of the Air Force. The Air Force planes also supplied the religious missions that for several years had painstakingly installed themselves along the river bends, a service that created deep and mutual respect between the two institutions. The Indian Protection Service, later renamed FUNAI – National Indian Foundation, was another organization that grew supported by the CAN. If it weren't for the Brazilian Air Force, several important development un-

Perfect for operations in the Amazon, the C-115 Buffalo was instrumental in the opening of new runways, which were useable only to aircraft capable of very short takeoffs and landings. Good for these strips, the Buffalo would carry machines and materials for the expansion of the runways. Upon completion, they could take larger planes such as C-130 Hercules transports. The photo on the facing page shows a Buffalo belonging to the 1st/9th Aviation Group, Arará (Macaw) Squadron flying over the famous meeting of the waters, where the Negro and Solimões Rivers join. (Pages 80/81) The runway at Cachimbo suddenly appears out of the jungle like an aircraft carrier out at sea. The COMARA has completed over 870 kilometers of runways throughout the Amazon, a distance equivalent to the road between Rio de Janeiro and Curitiba.

dertakings such as the Central Brazil Foundation and later the Rondon Project, would never have occurred.

With the consolidation of the CAN in the Amazon, the entire country had been linked by air. The international routes were also routine. In 1957 a line was open to the Middle East where the Suez Battalion of the Brazilian Army participated in the UN peacekeeping efforts in that part of the Globe. Four engined B-17 Flying Fortresses of the 6th Aviation Group and later the C-54Gs of the 1st/2nd Transport Group crossed the Atlantic to Europe and then to the Middle East with supplies for the troops. This Line was operational for more than 10 years. In 1960, Lines were opened to Buenos Aires and Santiago. And it was in that same year that Brasilia; the new National Capital was inaugurated in the heart of the country. The Airmail Service aircraft were instrumental in building the great city that like them also pointed to the west and the integration of the country's outback. Located some 1,200 kilometers from the coast, Brasilia had to be supplied by air. Thousands of tons of construction materials, machines and passengers were airlifted by the Air Force, whose pilots had to spot the clouds of red dust lifted by the tractors in frantic construction work and that spiraled upwards with the hot thermals of the Central Plateau. At that time the FAB had begun receiving aircraft with larger cargo holds, such as the C-54s, the C-82s and the C-119, this last one known as the Flying Boxcar. The arrival of these airplanes allowed the implementation of the Trunk Lines that operated from the established ones and reached new runways further inland. The C-47s were mostly moved to the Amazon where they expanded the tonnage in cargo and passengers carried annually by the Airmail Service.

The growth in the number of aircraft flying in Brazilian airspace brought the consolidation of a modern air traffic control system developed by the Flight Protection Service (SPV). Airways were demarcated, high power beacons were implanted, and well-trained professionals began controlling the traffic in the skies above Brazil.

In the early 60s the Airmail Service pilots had a general view of the level of development the country was going through. Their view was not restricted to the incredible advancement that was occurring in the southeastern and southern regions. They looked at the country in its entirety, and thus, it came as no surprise when in 1965, the Minister of Aeronautics, Lieutenant General Nelson Freire Lavénère Wanderley signed the purchase order for the first of sixteen C-130 Hercules transports. Three years later, the FAB acquired 24 C-115 Buffalo STOL planes. Capable of carrying large payloads with efficiency never before witnessed in Brazil's transport aviation, the first were capable of radically increasing the tonnage of supplies arriving to the Amazon while the latter made sure they arrived at the advanced runways stranded in the middle of the bush. Capable of landing in very short runways, the Buffalo were crucial in the effort to build airfields in inaccessible yet essential locations. Shortly after the C-115s had done their work; new gravel runways could begin receiving C-130s that brought large asphalt plants and the materials necessary to pave the landing strips.

By 1956 the COMARA had devised a master plan for the construction of 54 airfields throughout the Amazon to provide the safe flight over the entire region. From the pioneer airfields to the large airports, the COMARA fought tenaciously against

---

It is not only over the jungle that the FAB patrols the skies. The vast maritime area stranding the Amazon coast is also a primary responsibility of the Air Force, especially for her maritime patrol units. In the case of the Amazon, the coast is patrolled by the 3rd/7th GAv, Netuno Squadron. From their base in Belém they scan the important waters that stretch from the Atlantic to the Caribbean Sea in search of fishing boats operating illegally in Brazilian waters as well as smugglers, ecological disasters and several different types of irregular traffic besides offering an excellent search and rescue capability.

the elements and the difficult topography but was tremendously successful and today, as active as always can boast of having built over 130 runways all over the Brazilian Amazon. Of these, few are not able to take large aircraft such as the C-130, and this marks the end of an era when Amazon operations required specialized planes such as the Catalinas and the Buffalo. Santarém, Altamira, Cachimbo, São Felix do Xingú, Itaituba, Jacareacanga, Marabá, Conceição do Araguaia, Tiriós, Tabatinga, Ipiranga, Estirão do Equador, Barcelos, Uaupés, Surucucu, Japurá, Cucuí, Rio Branco, Tarauacá, Porto Nacional, Guajará-Mirim, Oiapoque and many others are names that become better known every day. As the runways become operational, the neighboring settlements develop, becoming an integral part of Brazil in the jungle, as well as providing greater comfort to their inhabitants.

In 1971, the Air Force created the CECAN – Airmail Service Center - to organize the CAN system using the transport assets at its disposal. The aircraft used by the CAN, and that had been previously commanded by the large transport units, became subordinate to the 5th Air Force while those that belonged to the Air Transport Squadrons came under the command of their respective Regional Air Commands. With the CAN completely solidified, and its lines taking progress to the people of the Brazilian North, the Air Force began looking at its other primary mission which is the defense of the vast jungle area. At any moment, its transport units could be called upon to move military units to the Amazon providing a rapid reaction capability in response to any unexpected act that might threaten the nation.

A new plane started equipping the FAB squadrons in 1973. Produced in large numbers by Embraer, the EMB-110 Bandeirante is a twin engined low wing, simple yet robust platform that came to prove Casemiro Montenegro's theory that Brazil could produce aircraft in large numbers to equip its air force. After building the Bandeirante, Embraer designed the Xingú, a pressurized plane used to transport a small number of passengers and for multiengine training. The next step was the EMB-120 Brasilia, a larger plane than the Bandeirante, capable of carrying a greater payload in cargo or in passengers and equipped with far more advanced avionics.

In 1973, Brazil saw the implantation of the first CINDACTA – *Centro Integrado de Defesa Aérea e Controle do Tráfego Aéreo,* Integrated Air Defense and Air Traffic Control Center – a radar network monitored by a control center responsible for the entire operation of both civil and military aircraft in the country. This was a unique approach to air traffic control, which went to show the deep concern that the leaders of the Brazilian Air Force had with the complete integration of the country's airspace.

On the threshold of the 21st Century, the Brazilian Amazon is completely integrated by air. Air Force aircraft share the airspace over the forest with civilian planes of all sizes and registries. From the large commercial airliners, to the regional planes from local companies and even the small single engine planes the crisscross the lower altitudes in every direction, their numbers increase as years go by. However, while most of Brazil is under a complex system of aerospace protection, the Amazon was until recently, devoid of efficient radar coverage capable of allowing effective control over its skies.

Flying over the Amazon is like flying over the vastness of the oceans. There are practically no landing spots on most routes. On the facing page an UH-1H of the 7th/8th GAv admires the Green Hell from above.
(Pages 88/89) All of the missions flown in the Amazon are operational as they occur in extremely rugged areas. The aircraft used by the Air Force in the jungle strips must be extremely resistant, as this Embraer C-95B of the 1st Air Transport Squadron taking off from an unpaved runway.

SUPPORTING THOSE WHO FLY
CONTROLLING BRAZIL'S AIRSPACE

Today a Rio-São Paulo flight may be merely a routine for Brazilian flyers. However, the advances seen since Montenegro and Wanderley's historic flight, only seven decades ago, show how air traffic control grew and developed in Brazil. Flown with no external support and with rudimentary maps, the first Airmail Service flight was considered a great adventure. When the military aviators of those days started flying to the interior, they began travelling to regions where there weren't even any roads to help them navigate. It didn't take them long, however, to developed a new way to fly.

EYES WIDE OPEN

Because of the lack of major landmarks, the pilots of the old Curtiss biplanes opted to fly nap of the Earth, *glued to the ground*, as they would say, while they followed the few railroads that ventured towards the outback. It was what they called *Railroad Navigation*. For that they used an instrument then considered even more essential than the airspeed indicator, altimeters and other dials that equipped their instrument panels. It was jokingly called the *eyemeter*, the only instrument capable of keeping the vital railroad tracks within sight! The young pilots used to say that; "*The compass is in your neck and that sometimes it had to be massaged so that it wouldn't malfunction!*" If bad weather was encountered and the clouds descended to lower levels, the aviators did everything

they could not to lose sight of the tracks, even if they entered what they mockingly called *farsighted flight*, and which was neither blind nor visual. In case they lost sight of the ground the only solution would be to land anywhere they could, rather than risk getting lost or flying into a mountainous region. And when they landed they had to be extremely careful, as there were no airfields. The pilots had to pick a suitable field, survey it as best they could under the pressing circumstances and land safely making sure they didn't crash land which could destroy the planes as well as the pilots themselves. This style of flying was called *pecking* as the Airmail pilots learned to dive amidst the low clouds, sometimes circling around them or keeping below them making sure they never lost ground reference, much like a chicken stooping to feed. Many times they landed near railroad stations to use the telegraph to gather information about the weather situation on the route ahead.

The resourcefulness demonstrated by Lieutenant Faria Lima in painting signs on the roofs of railroad stations and churches, helped his companions navigate to their destinations, but more important, it constituted the first effort to create an effective support system for air transport in Brazil.

BUILDING THE NETWORK

When the Second World War reached Brazil, the young Airmail pilots had vast experience in flying under adverse conditions and excelled in every new mission which was introduced to them. The ferrying of aircraft from the United States to Brazil, the long maritime patrol missions over the coast and the Atlantic, the fighter-bomber and artillery spotting missions on the Italian Theatre of Operations all contributed to boost the nascent Brazilian Air

Since its inception in 1941, the Brazilian Air Force has dedicated itself to build highly operational civilian as well as military aviation sectors. The professionalism of several generations of Air Force officers helped create an air transport network with safety standards comparable to those of North America and Europe. (Pages 92/93) Concentrated on the several blips appearing on his radar console, an Air Force flight controller scans the air scene at one of the country's several CINDACTA Area Control Centers- ACC.

Force to an early maturity. While in the United States, Brazilian pilots witnessed the advances in technique and equipment necessary to the conduction of air traffic control in an atmosphere where the skies were crowded with airplanes on their way and coming from training facilities or being ferried to the war zones.

The same equipments and techniques were brought by the US forces to the Brazilian Northeast, lest the huge amount of air traffic leaving and arriving from North Africa develop into daily accidents. Parnamirim Base, near Natal in Rio Grande do Norte was so crowded that for several years it was the second busiest Allied base in the number of takeoffs and landings per day. The American experience in organizing their airspace was observed and adopted by the Brazilian Air Force, soon being used to benefit the Airmail Service operations. Control towers, stronger radio beacon stations, better radios and communication procedures, the establishment of airways, the adoption of instrument climb and approach procedures near the airfield terminal areas and the organization of flight instruction and publishing of flight manuals all helped regulate Brazilian aviation. It was the end of the era of adventure flying, always near the ground which typified the country's aviation until then. At the close of World War II, a large number of C-47 and DC-3 airplanes were acquired not only by the Air Force but also by several commercial airlines, resulting in ever growing congestion in the skies. Eduardo Gomes made good use of the experience he gathered while commanding the FAB in the northeast, implementing the Flight Protection Service in the early 50's. This service was created to provide support to aerial navigation in an organized and well structured way. It was during this time that Brazil acquired its first radar station which was promptly installed at Santa Cruz Air Base and used to train the pilots of the new Gloster Meteor fighters in air interception techniques. In 1956 the first VOR – Very High Frequency Omni Range was affixed at the locality of Duque de Caxias in the terminal approach area to Rio's Galeão Airport. The VORs emit Hertzian waves whose signals are received inside the aircraft cockpits, showing the direction of flight, distance to the next beacon, groundspeed and consequently the time to destiny. Distant CAN stations were provided with Flight Protection Detachments which allowed around the clock operation in practically any weather conditions. The communications and flight safety equipment on the ground were manned and maintained by specialists that resided at the airfields guaranteeing nonstop service. These equipments needed regular checking and for that purpose, the Air Force contracted the services of a flight inspection aircraft from the CAA – U.S. Civil Aviation Authority in 1956. Aircraft for that mission were already being fitted for FAB use. In 1958, two Brazilian officers were sent to the United States where they received training as inspector pilots, and on that same year the first laboratory aircraft arrived in Brazil. In February 1959, the first inspection flight was finally flown by a Brazilian aircraft and crew.

Flying in Brazil was becoming less of an adventure as years went by. In the early sixties Galeão Airport, then the principal gateway to the country, received the first of several ILS transmitters. The Instrument Landing System – ILS – allows an aircraft on approach to follow a veritable electronic path until it is perfectly aligned with the runway for landing. Galeão also received an ALS – Approach and Landing System which uses different color lights to provide incoming pilots with a simple visualization of the ideal landing ramp. The dedication of the Brazilian Air Force to the regulation of its growing air system soon turned the country into a reference for aerial operations in Latin America. Always well informed about what was happening at the forefront of the air traffic control and safety activities around the world, the FAB would soon implant a new system which would be considered a revolutionary example of efficiency.

THE BIRTH OF CINDACTA

In 1973, Lieutenant-General Joelmir Campos de Araripe Macedo, then Minister of Aeronautics, implemented a system called CINDACTA – Centro Integrado de Defesa Aérea e Controle do Tráfego Aéreo – Integrated Air De-

(Pages 96/97) Throughout the extensive Brazilian territory, several radar stations such as this one located atop Pico do Couto, near the city of Petrópolis, west of Rio de Janeiro, guarantee the control of the country's airspace. Linked in a complex network, they furnish real-time monitoring of aerial contacts, allowing the authorities to track every aircraft flying over its skies. Little by little the Brazilian Air Force succeeded in providing radar coverage to a large part of its territory.

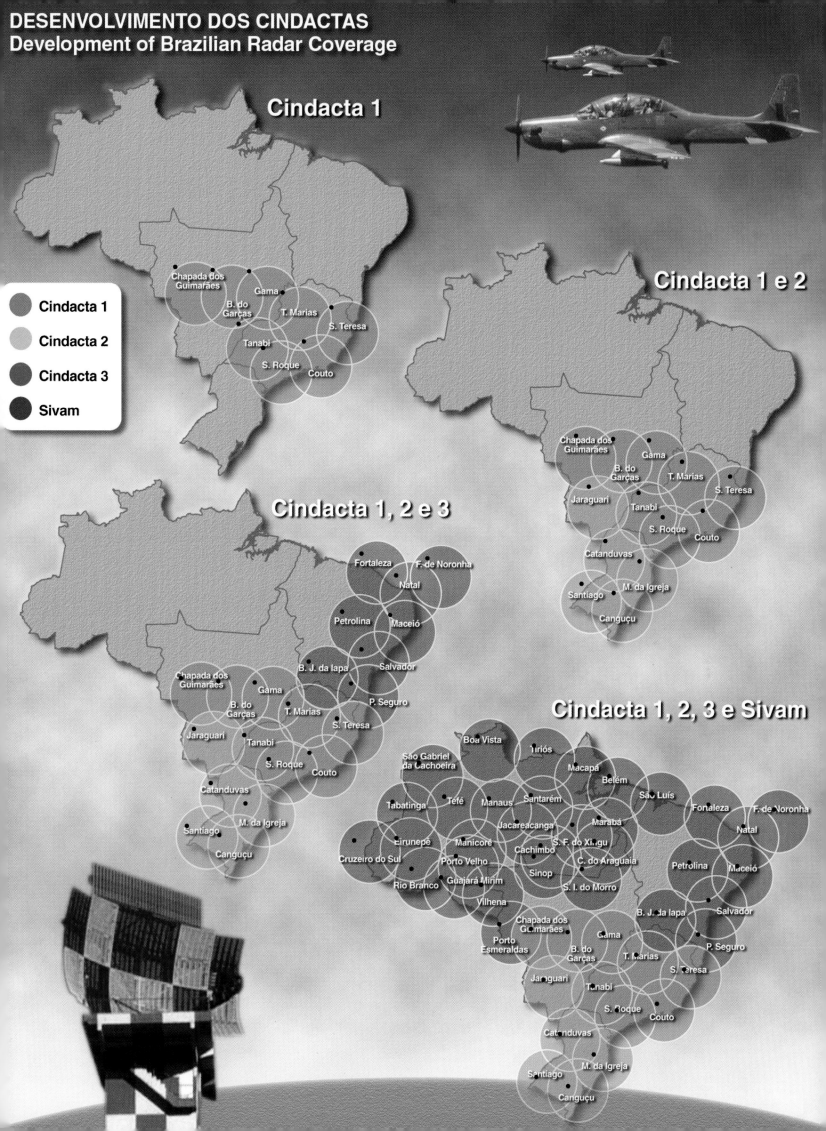

DESENVOLVIMENTO DOS CINDACTAS
Development of Brazilian Radar Coverage

fense and Air Traffic Control Center, a revolutionary system which combined civil and military operations under a single control network. A system of radars and control centers spread around the country would provide the Ministry with the position of every aircraft overflying Brazil at a given moment in real time. Originally from the first generation of Airmail Service pilots, General Araripe Macedo was another of the important pillars of the efficient aeronautical infrastructure built in Brazil by a generation that intimately felt the difficulty of flying over the country's vast expanses. With the creation of the CINDACTA, the Air Force would continue on its mission to develop Brazil's aviation, providing the same conditions to civilian aircraft as it used for its own planes. The first unit was CINDACTA I based in Brasilia and that covered the most congested areas in the southeastern and central regions. Then came CINDACTA II, with an Area Control Center in Curitiba, and covering the southern portion of the country. Away from the public eye, the Air Force worked hard, building radar stations in spots that were as inaccessible as necessary. Little by little the system which would eventually provide complete radar coverage over Brazilian airspace was put together. The third phase, CINDACTA III was erected next in Recife on the northeastern shores, stretching the system to the major American and European approach routes to the nation's main cities.

Once a flight plan is telexed to the aeronautical authorities by airlines, military commands and general aviation pilots, a computer analysis of the desired route is made. Once the flight is approved it is sent directly to the control tower of the destination airport as well as to the approach center that commands the destination's approach proceedures. During its flight the aircraft is tracked by the radars that line its route transmitting their signals to the centers to which they belong. The radarscope operator sees not only the airplane in question but all others

To ensure that the air navigation equipment such as radars, VOR beacons, ILS transmitters and approach and landing lights are functioning smoothly, the Air Force is equipped with a squadron which is specialized in inspecting them and that flies missions around the clock over the country's entire territory. Airplanes such as this HS-125 as well as several Embraer EMB-110 Bandeirante fitted with special equipment fly yearly inspection campaigns both in Brazil and in several neighboring countries. (Pages 100/101) FAB flight controllers are handpicked to guarantee the highest safety standards.

around it. At any given moment a pilot can be informed of the conditions around him.

On the same year that the CINDACTA was born, the Air Force also created the GEIV – *Grupo Especial de Inspeção em Vôo*, Special Flight Inspection Group – a squadron equipped with Embraer EMB-110 Bandeirantes and HS-125s filled with equipment capable of checking the VOR, ILS, NDB – Non-Directional Radio Beacon – DME – Distance Measuring Equipment, ALS – Approach Lighting System, VASIS – Visual Approach Slope Indicator System, PAPIS – Precision Approach Path Indicator as well as the several PAR – Precision Approach Radars located on the several airports and air bases throughout the country.

The long, silent and arduous work of the Brazilian Air Force in creating a well-integrated system, ensured that the control of Brazilian airspace went from the rudimentary control of aircraft in flight using the positioning informed by radio to controllers on the ground, to the complex integrated system that permits that any aircraft flying over a given area be observed and controlled by specialized personnel. This was the SISCEAB – *Sistema de Controle do Espaço Aéreo Brasileiro*, Brazilian Airspace Control System – finally consolidated.

In the early 90's most of Brazil was covered by the CINDACTA. The only region left uncovered was the Amazon. With radars operating only at Manaus, Belém, Boa Vista and on the border with Colombia and Peru where the action of drug smugglers demanded an emergency installation of two radar sites at Tabatinga (AM) and São Gabriel da Cachoeira (AM), the rest of the Brazilian Amazon was left unguarded. The lack of control over the region also brought uneasy feelings to many in the commercial air traffic that had to fly virtually blindfolded over a large part of the continent. The military pilots would sometimes say in jest that over the Amazon they would fly VOR, or *Visually Over the Rivers!* Once the CINDACTA I, II and III were completed the Air Force finally turned its attention to the last – and certainly most challenging – region over which it would have to establish conditions for the proper control of Brazilian air traffic. The first step of a long journey had been taken. One of the most ambitious programs ever undertaken by Brazil had been set in motion, the SIPAM/SIVAM Project, the final arrival of the Brazilian Nation to the skies of the Amazon.

PRESENCE ON THE LAST FRONTIER
THE SIPAM/SIVAM PROJECT

In the early nineties the Brazilian Amazon was totally integrated by the Air Force. Its aircraft reached every airfield and airport throughout the great forest. Army detachments dotted the national limits, providing protection where the country begins. Navy ships sailed the rivers monitoring strategic passages as well as providing medical and social help to the most distant localities rarely reached by civilization.

There was however, still a lot to do in the Amazon. Brazil needed to know the forest better, protect its resources, defend its sovereignty and improve the living conditions of the Brazilians that resided in the country's furthermost region. Brazil wanted to take better care of its portion of the Amazon. And it came as no surprise that the decision to implement a new organized, rational and well-structured plan would come exactly from those who knew the region best; the men of the Brazilian Air Force.

In the first few months of 1990 the Ministry of Aeronautics, along with the SAE -Directorate of Strategic Affairs and the Ministry of Justice presented Exposition of Motives number 194 to the Presidency. Its objective was to create a complex system that would guarantee an effective vigilance and protection of the Amazon Region. The several steps taken since the first Airmail Service flight on

Technology finally comes to the great forest! With the arrival of the SIPAM/SIVAM Project, the Brazilian Air Force will begin to control every flight that passes over the Amazon as it does throughout the rest of the country.

that distant June 12, almost six decades earlier needed yet another. It was the birth of the SIVAM Project – The Amazon Vigilance System. The Brazilian Government had announced its firm intention to finally become the guardian of the great forest.

THE PROJECT IS CONSOLIDATED

The first step in implementing the new project, was a presentation by the coalition of interested government bodies, of the myriad problems that affected not only the region, but the entire country. Smugglers and drug traffickers used the porous northern and northwestern borders bringing weapons, narcotics and industrial products that would be sold on the market without the payment of taxes normally charged upon the entrance to the country. Shipments of several sizes arrived by air, and through the rivers only to disappear in the immense jungle, reappearing later in the great Brazilian cities or finding their way to the seaports where they could be smuggled yet again to the promising markets of North America and Europe. Amazonian resources such as birds, fish and tropical animals, noble woods and the thousands of genetic products found in the jungle are also smuggled albeit in the opposite direction and with no benefit for the region's people. Worse still, many of its prime resources which are composed of ingredients taken from the heart of the forest, especially those that feed the pharmaceutical industry, return to the Brazilian market to be sold for exorbitant prices. It was important that the Brazilian Government create an integrated vigilance coordination capacity uniting all the means at its disposal to curtail illegal actions both in the Amazon as well as those originating from it.

The unfamiliarity with what occurred in a large portion of the forest also worried the members of the several government agencies that were trying to have the project approved by the President. For centuries, Brazil's inhabitants, were kept uninformed of the scientific discoveries made by the great researchers that roamed the country's outback. Few imagined the vast resources that lay deep in the jungle. To benefit from the scientific research that several companies and nations had been sponsoring for years and which reverted to their economic advancement, Brazil had to know the Amazon as never before.

Finally, the program should bring progress, development and comfort to the growing population of Brazil's northern states. The great effort made by the Airmail Service to reach its distant populations had not been forgotten. Now, with technology on its side and with a definite commitment to develop the green region, the Government was finally prepared to further integrate it to the rest of the country.

Under the leadership of the organizations that started the project, the government was finally ready to provide a system that would allow all of its agencies to act in an integrated manner in the Amazon.

On September 21, 1990 the exposition of motives was finally approved by the President, and the race was on. SAE would prepare a national co-ordination system, merging all government agencies into one extremely efficient network. The information generated by the program would be distributed according to each organ's specific needs.

The Ministry of Aeronautics, comprising several experts on the region, would be responsible for the implementation and management of the programs' assets. It would also respond for its operation. The Ministry of Justice would provide legal backing, allowing the several law enforcement agencies involved to act against any illegal deeds in the area.

By the end of the decade, something was afoot in Brazil. From the FAB pilots accustomed to observe aircraft used by smugglers flying unimpeded over the forest without being able to do much, to the scientists, aware of the different components of important formulas commercialized overseas with ingredients taken from the banks of the rivers. From the diplomats who were tired of hearing that their country was the source of the Planet's ecological misfortunes, to the Indians, who have been manipulated by the most varied interest groups to take one or another stance which would do nothing but bring economic advantages for the groups involved. Even the peaceful inhabitants of the forest, spread throughout the rubber plantations, the mountain ranges and villages, trading posts and industrial projects and in little houses on stilts by the river sides. Everyone seemed to sense that a new era was arriving. The Brazilian Air Force had not forgotten them. With its operational runways all over the forest, its squadrons making sure that the flow of supplies and passengers continued, and its leaders keeping the vow of their forebears, it was finally ready for the next and perhaps most ambitious stage of its lifelong contest; to consolidate the Amazon once and for all.

One of the tasks of the SIPAM/SIVAM is the creation of a giant database to study the meteorological conditions over the Amazon Basin. The effects of lightning and of its resulting electromagnetic pulses are among the principal phenomena to be studied, mostly for the benefit of air traffic safety. (Pages 106/107) The race is on! The SIPAM/SIVAM Project is being implemented at great speed. Sites are blossoming throughout the entire Brazilian Amazon. The picture portrays construction work at the Manaus Regional Vigilance Center. This complex will concentrate every information generated by the several sensors spread throughout the forest, interacting with the other centers at Manaus and Porto Velho.

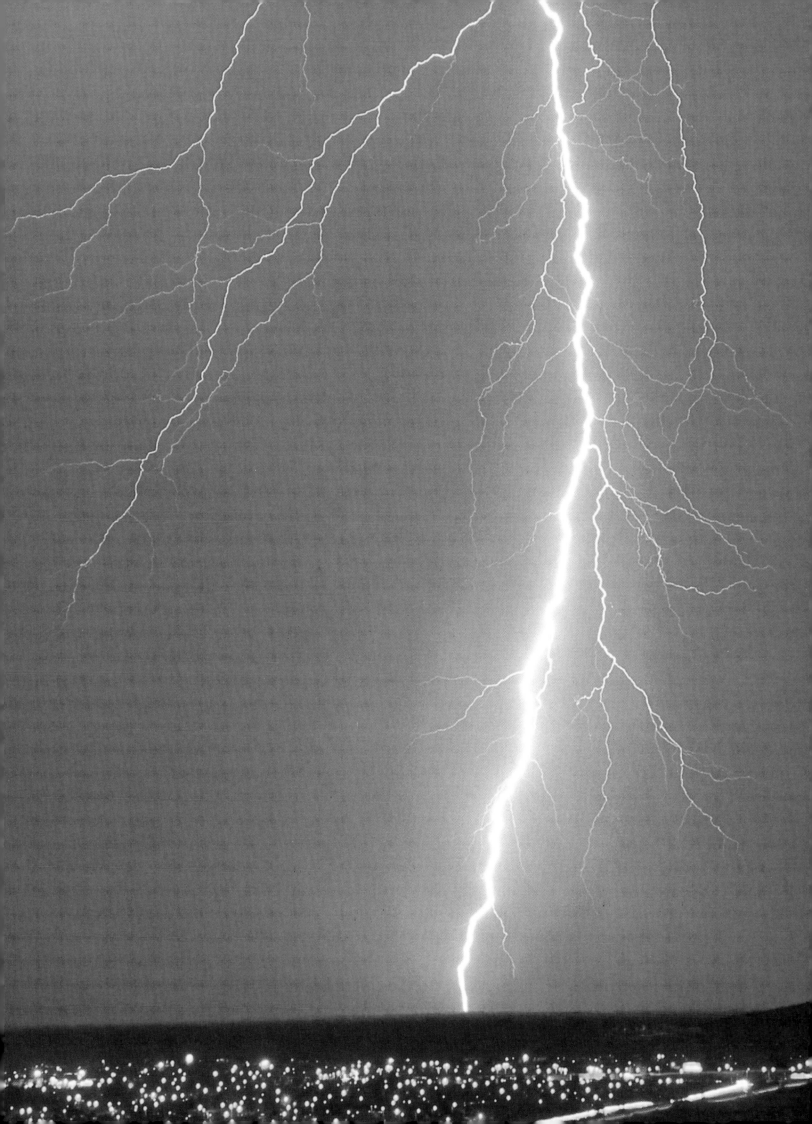

THE SHAPING OF SIVAM

To head the actions that would eventually shape the SIVAM and the National Coordination System, whose name was soon changed to SIPAM – Amazon Protection System, the Air Force designated a very special man. An extremely intelligent and hard working officer, General Marcos Antonio de Oliveira, from the town of Araxá in Minas Gerais, immediately went to work by personally selecting his team. He hand-picked excellent Air Force officers assigning them to their new jobs according to their personal characteristics. In a short time his crew was formed and the guidelines ready. Five years after the first move, the SIVAM would become operational.

The project would consume a total of US$ 1.4 billion, in external financing payable within 20 years. The only thing missing was the difficult political cohesion that would guarantee national support for the project. The economic occupation of any area always encounters strong resistance and SIVAM soon met the opposition of interest groups that had been extracting resources from the forest for years. The large amounts involved in the purchase of equipment and services also mobilized companies and governments ready to do battle for a part of the important contract. Unfamiliar with the nuances and even the importance of the project for the benefit of the country, a good portion of the public opinion was ambivalent regarding the controversy that it generated in all strata of society. Faced with all sorts of obstacles, General Oliveira and his team kept a steady and firm heading, always following the determination of the Air Force, while pushing SIVAM forward a step at a time. Each of the program's goals was met until it was definitely approved, defined, understood and ready to move forward.

THE GOVERNMENT WORKING AS ONE

SIVAM's major objective is to take the Federal Government as a single, active and compact block, and make it present in the Brazilian Amazon. What finally made this presence possible was the massive advent of information technology that appeared in the last two decades of the 20th Century. Before that, the transmission of information and knowledge demanded a permanent physical presence, which the Brazilian Government was unable to provide due to its constant budgetary privations. Until then, the country's occupancy of the Amazon was almost the sole privilege of the Armed Forces who were practically the only institutions devoted to the mission of pioneering the region. With the advent of state-of-the-art telecommunications and the arrival of the digital era, distances became smaller and the transmission of data and information in real-time became a daily occurrence. SIVAM made use of these technologies to integrate the several government institutions with Amazonian responsibilities.

Throughout the Amazon, the Air Force is installing 25 telecommunications sites, meteorological surface and altitude stations, mobile and fixed vigilance radars and VHF transmitters. Called Vigilance Units, they are located at the cities of: Boa Vista (Roraima), São Gabriel da Cachoeira, Tabatinga, Manaus, Manicoré, Tefé, and Eirunepé (Amazonas), Jacareacanga, Cachimbo, Belém, Santarém, Marabá, São Felix do Xingú and Conceição do Araguaia (Pará), Santa Isabel do Morro, Sinop and Porto Espiridião (Mato Grosso), Porto Velho, Vilhena, and Guajará-Mirim (Rondônia), Rio Branco and Cruzeiro do Sul (Acre), Tiriós and Macapá (Amapá) and São Luís (Maranhão).

Besides the Vigilance Units, the SIVAM also incorporates Telecommunications Units equipped with voice, text and image transferring equipment

The planned construction of the SIPAM/SIVAM Project sites followed a rigorous schedule, and soon the great towers that sustain the fixed radar antennae such as this one at Rio Branco, Acre, began to reach for the skies.

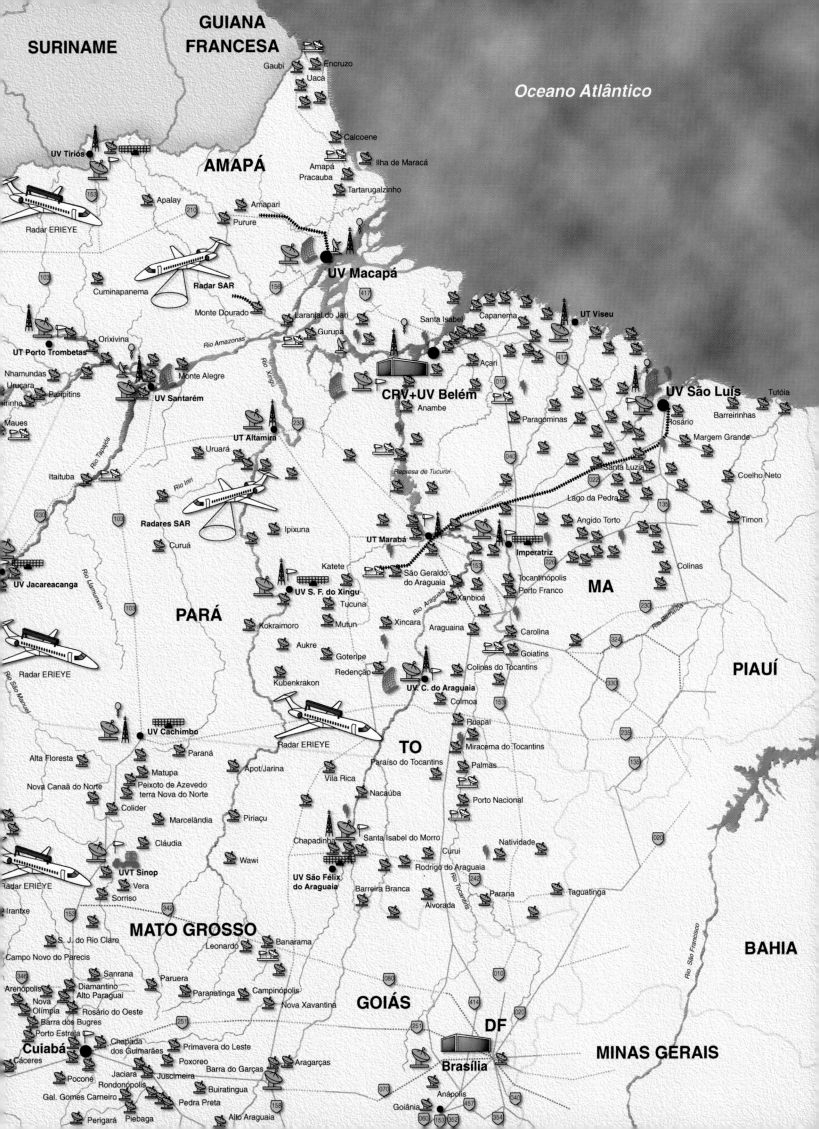

which will be used to transmit data to the several users of the project. This data, which will also be produced and consumed by local government users will be processed by three Regional Vigilance Centers (CRV) located at Manaus in Amazonas, Belém in Pará and Porto Velho in Rondônia. The information generated by these centers will be pertinent to the regional government offices, but will be passed along to the General Coordination Center in Brasilia, the major headquarters for the entire system.

The SIVAM will not only monitor, collect and process data about the region but will also have the ability to act whenever necessary. Data acquisition will come from a multitude of sensors spread throughout the jungle, in the skies and in space. Two types of information are of interest to the system. The environmental data – that will be collected to enable the government to build a database with which to study the region's delicate climatic situation – and the vigilance data - that allows the system's users to monitor any actions that may endanger Brazil's sovereignty over the area.

To collect the environmental figures, SIVAM utilizes several satellites (TIROS, GOES/METEOSAT, SCD-1, LANDSAT, SPOT, CBERS and ERS-1) that send information from space directly to the local CRVs or to INPE – National Space Research Institute. It also uses specialized aircraft equipped with synthetic aperture radars as well as with multispectral sensors. These are extremely effective at lower altitudes and can collect images below the

A Xavante Indian admires the vast Amazonian landscape of rivers and forest through the window of a C-115 transport. The Brazilian Indians, supported by the Air Force for generations will benefit immensely by the arrival of the new system. Conscious of the need to better the living conditions of Brazil's indigenous populations, the Brazilian Government has been striving to make sure that tribes that have had contact with progress be given the opportunity to partake of the comforts of civilization. (Pages 114/115) Another major function of the SIPAM/SIVAM Project is the collection of knowledge that will allow Brazil to control the evasion of biological resources that are smuggled from the jungle in great quantities. Brazilian scientists will use the system to conduct research as has been happening with many scientists whose work is sponsored by several nations and companies.

clouds, which are commonplace in the Amazon. Ten meteorological radars monitor cloud formations around the clock, while surface and altitude data collecting units constantly monitor the several layers of the atmosphere over the jungle. The altitude data collecting units, numbering thirteen, send instruments to great atmospheric heights to create a database capable of determining weather patterns which will be used to make air transport over the region safer. Temperature, wind direction and intensity in the several layers, atmospheric pressure and its effects on the region's rains, as well as on the levels of pollution and ozone present in the atmosphere will be monitored closely. This data will not only help Brazilian scientists understand the region better, but will also be available to the international scientific community. Seventy surface data collecting units will operate in the same manner, but on the ground. Temperature, winds, atmospheric pressure, rainfall and solar radiation and their effects on the ground will also be analyzed scientifically. These stations will be complemented by a network of 200 data collecting platforms spread throughout the entire Brazilian Amazon and whose reports will be immediately linked to all interested parties connected to the intricate telecommunications net. This vast web of sensors will bring an enormous amount of scientific information that should influence the preservation of the region's ecosystem. It will monitor the size of the jungle canopy, forest fires, the results and extent of pollution in the rivers, occasional epidemics, preserved Indian areas, and of the correct usage of developed land capable of bettering the lives of the local population.

The other information collected and controlled by the system is the vigilance data, which allows for an increase of the region's control by the Brazilian Government. These are also produced by satellites and aircraft and are complemented by communications exploration and direction finding

equipment that allow the authorities to monitor not only the aerial, terrestrial, riverine and maritime movements, but the communications between clandestine and criminal groups operating in the jungle area.

Composed of 936 kits equipped with laptop computers, fax machines, and small Satcom antennae, this intelligence when collated, will offer a detailed picture of what is currently happening in the Amazon. It can be accessed by any agency directly involved in the area such as the Army, the Navy, FUNAI, Ibama, the Federal Police as well as local government, both city or state.

THE IMPROVEMENT OF THE AIR TRAFFIC CONTROL STRUCTURE

There are few places on Earth where aircraft cannot be monitored from the ground at all times: the oceans, parts of the great deserts, the frozen expanses of the poles and the Amazon Region.

Flying over the Amazon is the equivalent to overflying the oceans. There are few places to land in the event of an emergency. The runways built in the jungle appear much like islands in the sea, and are a blessed sight to pilots with problems. During the last 50 years, the COMARA was able to sprinkle over one hundred airfields throughout the Amazon, enormously reducing the distances between a landing and another. This arduous and rarely recognized effort improved the safety for all aircraft flying over the region, and offered a larger number of options for pilots facing malfunctions. However, despite the fact that Brazil is covered by a network of radars belonging to the CINDACTA, the Amazon remained practically in the dark in what concerns air traffic control and air navigation safety. With the SIVAM this giant void is finally being covered. Fixed, mobile and airborne radars and meteorological monitoring systems provide information about the conditions of the air-

space in real time. Air navigation equipment and inspection aircraft checking them, will interact to ensure that the skies over the Amazon can be monitored around the clock becoming a place where aircraft of all sizes and types can fly safely. The air traffic control system will be integrated to the CINDACTAs I and III based in Brasilia and Recife, their data being fused to provide the tracking of a single airplane during its flight throughout the entire Brazilian landmass. The information gathered by this system will also be available at the CRVs at Manaus, Belém and Porto Velho as well as at the CCG in Brasilia. Four new ILS – Instrument Landing System sets have been bought for the airports at Boa Vista, Santarém, Cuiabá and Porto Velho, an acquisition that will increase the safety of final approach and landing operations at these airports, especially at night or in bad weather. These cities are situated within the ITCZ – Intertropical Convergence Zone, an area that straddles the Planet around the Equator and that suffers a larger proportion of foul weather days than other areas of the Globe, demanding greater care in flight operations. Besides, 32 telecommunications sites increase the number of localities capable of supporting aircraft in flight over the region. Operating via satellite and powered by solar energy, they will guarantee the integration of isolated localities bringing great benefit to local air traffic.

The Area Control Center at Manaus, which is the principal air traffic control center in the Amazon, is being modernized to adapt to the great

Pressurized and with better performance and payload than the Bandeirante, the Embraer EMB-120 Brasilia operates with great efficiency in the Amazon. (Pages 118/119) Perhaps the most important yet most forgotten localities in the Amazon are the border posts manned by Army personnel and supplied by the Air Force, such as the distant runway at Surucucu on the border with Venezuela. Besides being the first line to sound an alarm, the border detachments are also an important factor for the country's integration. It is also possible that the reason why Portuguese is spoken throughout such a vast territory, is due to the dedicated work of the men who live in such distant places guarding the borders. Relaxing in the cargo hold of a C-115 of the 1st/9th Aviation Group, a platoon of Army men fly towards their post.

changes that are rapidly occurring. New data processing equipment and modern displays allow a better man-machine-interface aiding the controllers to better understand the air traffic control picture unfolding before them at any given time. As soon as it becomes operationally tested, the new system will also equip the area control centers located at the other CINDACTA headquarters.

To ensure the perfect functioning of the equipment being installed for the SIPAM/SIVAM, the Air Force took delivery of four new HS-800XP jets equipped with automatic inspection consoles which allow them to conduct the inspection of signals emanating from ground based air navigation equipment without the need for autonomous ground teams. Operated by the GEIV – Special Flight Inspection Group, the four new planes will make sure that the system is always properly maintained, contributing to the safety of pilots and passengers cruising over the forest or using local airports. With the arrival of the SIVAM, flying over the Amazon has suddenly become an extremely safe routine and no longer the great adventure that it once was. This brings greater comfort not only to the large jets flying on the airways, thousands of feet above the Earth, but to the airlines who own them, as it reduces the costs charged by insurance companies for flights over non-monitored areas. It also makes life difficult to those who conduct illegal or irregular air activities that not only threaten the country's economic integrity but bring great risks to day by day air operations. Controlling these flights will provide a better psychological feeling to pilots and passengers who now know they are being monitored as they fly over what was once known as the Green Hell.

THE WINGS OF THE SIVAM

Throughout the years the Airmail Service brought air transport to the region. Now, the Amazon is being integrated electronically. The increase in scientific knowledge about the region, the monitoring of the environment as well as of the actions which offend the country's economy along with the government's capability to act against illicit activities will dramatically change life in the big forest. Yet perhaps the most visible aspect of SIPAM/SIVAM is in the skies of the Amazon.

Instead of asking for external help to combat the threat posed by drug traffickers and smugglers, Brazil has decided to act. The Brazilian Air Force, long aware of the problems it would someday face in the region, is finally receiving an interesting array of specialized aircraft with which it can curb the excessive liberty that allows a veritable swarm of air smugglers to fly over the huge yet largely unpatrolled border.

Five Embraer ERJ-145SA, airborne early warning and control aircraft designated R-99A by the FAB will complement the coverage of the 25 ground radars that are being installed to bring an effective control over the Amazon skies. Every aircraft flying over the region will be tracked and followed, their flight plans confirmed and authorized. However, even with this capacity, any aircraft flying below 10,000 feet will escape their observation. Most of the smaller planes used in illegal activities – which range from the smuggling of narcotics, weapons, and taxable goods coming in, while gold, precious minerals, Cash, exotic animals and resources of scientific value fly out – utilize these altitudes to escape from the vigilance of air traffic control.

Of these the most dangerous are the drug traffickers who, for several years have been picking

To ensure the perfect functioning of the air navigation systems that are being implemented in the Amazon, the GEIV – Special Flight Inspection Group is operating new HS-800 XP aircraft equipped with state of the art inspection equipment. (Pages 124/125) Throughout the Amazon Region, primary, secondary, autonomous and mobile radars are being installed. Operating together they will provide a compact image of most of the area's airspace above 10,000 feet.

different routes through Brazilian territory, while escaping from mounting pressure from the authorities of producing countries, Colombia, Peru and Bolivia. Drugs, mostly processed cocaine, is carried in small aircraft through the northern border trying to get to Manaus, Belém and the cities of the Brazilian southeast, where it can eventually be shipped to the major markets in Europe and in the United States. Flying scant feet above the canopy, frequently in bad weather and often in the darkness of night, they are targets, which are practically impossible to track with conventional radars. The R-99As, however, will change this situation. Equipped with an aerial planar array PS-890 Erieye radar, it can fly in complete silence searching for targets below, thus covering every flight level from its position downwards. Any airplane flying inside its detection range of some 350 kilometers will be interrogated in case its flight plan is not confirmed, or if flying in a suspicious manner. Inside the large rear cabin three systems operators will have complete control over giant portions of sky around them. Besides the radar picture, they will have at their disposal several signals intelligence systems, which will allow them to monitor distinct radio frequencies as well as unauthorized electronic emissions that are abundant over Northern Brazil. The plane, an ERJ-145 regional jet of the ER or Extended Range variant carries the 1,300-kg radar on piggyback over the fuselage. Its regular engines have been replaced by a more powerful version of the powerplant used in the regular ERJ-145s, the AE3007A1P. In the cabin, besides the two pilots and the three console operators, the plane can carry a replacement crew of five in comfortable accommodations allowing long mission legs.

Over 3,000 unauthorized aerial traffics occur every day throughout the 16.000 some kilometers that constitute the Brazilian border. These, range from the rancher whose airstrip is located only 15 minutes away from a friend's farm on the other side of the border, to those involving in illegal activities that damage the country's economy. Most of these flights do not issue flight plans, an extremely important document for the authorities that control Brazil's air traffic activities. When an R-99A crew detects an airplane without a flight plan in its area of responsibility, it immediately inquires its crew to learn what its intentions are. If these act in an unexpected way or if they try to escape, the radar plane will immediately scramble Embraer EMB-314 ALX light attack planes designated A-29 by the FAB. These robust planes which were developed from the famous EMB-312 Tucano trainer will permit efficient intercept operations in that part of the country. Fitted with a newer version of the PT6A engine and a Hartzell five bladed propeller, the A-29s will be superior if compared to the Tucano. At the same time, they will be able to operate on the same performance level as the small airplanes normally used by the traffickers. The A-29s will have state of the art digital avionics compatible with night vision goggles and FLIR Star Safire infrared cameras that will allow it to operate at night closing the window now used by the illegal flights.

In neighboring Peru the government has made every effort to blunt the traffickers flights using EMB-312 Tucanos specially equipped for the drug intercept mission. During the last few years the Fuerza Aerea Peruana has downed over 100 planes that have refused to obey orders to surrender or

Several mobile radars such as this one can be set up in specific areas where the coverage of the fixed sets is not complete, or in localities in which the equipment is momentarily unserviceable. Transported by airplane and helicopter, these radars will allow an extremely flexible coverage of large portions of sky.
(Pages 128/129) To detect targets flying below the levels (10,000ft) controlled by the SIPAM/SIVAM ground systems, the Brazilian Air Force operates Embraer ERJ-145SA airborne early warning and control aircraft designated R-99A. It will also fly Embraer ERJ-145RS or R-99B remote sensing craft. These planes are equipped with radars accommodated under the fuselage in special compartments to detect targets on the ground, as well as forest fires, deforestation and other phenomena that are presently monitored by satellite.

that adopted hostile actions against government planes. With the increment of FAP activity, the drug running flights became ever more dangerous resulting in a steep raise in the salaries of the few pilots willing to run the blockade. The smugglers then began flying in waves, in which only a few planes flew laden with drugs while the others tried to attract the authorities to fruitless searches in desolate runways hidden deep in the Peruvian Amazon. Soon, the FAP found ways to beat these tactics augmenting its patrols as well as intensifying intelligence on the ground. The reaction of the drug gangs was to fly at night, forcing the Peruvian Air Force to adapt to a new reality.

Knowing the details of this veritable silent war being waged over the jungles of Northern South America, the Brazilian Air Force is acquiring every available technology to block the passage of the smugglers through Brazilian territory. The A-29s are armed with two 12.7mm machine guns as well as GIAT NC621, 20mm cannons in pods under each wing. They also carry CTA/Mectron MAA-1 Piranha infrared missiles as well as conventional, laser guided and cluster bombs, a combination which also makes it effective against irregular military forces such as foreign guerrilla

---

The vastness of the Amazon jungle has allowed for the free passage of aircraft carrying products of illegal nature. These may be exotic birds, tropical fish, plants, roots and seeds of genetic value, industrialized products, Cash, precious stones, gold and many other resources that leave the Brazilian borders on a daily basis. On the opposite direction fly aircraft carrying contraband, drugs and weapons which will be sold in Brazil or in other markets in neighboring countries, Europe and North America and which are reached from the country's ports. The Brazilian Amazon is literally dotted with small clandestine airstrips from which a veritable armada of aircraft of all sizes operates without the acquiescence of the authorities.
(Pages 132/133) For several years the Brazilian Air Force has been trying to develop an interception doctrine against low performance planes. It has tried to use its high performance fighters such as the Mirage and F-5E but has not had good results. Concluding that it needed vectors compatible with the aircraft that conduct most of the smuggling flights, the Air Force decided to use armed versions of the Tucano trainer. The AT-27 Tucanos operate from Boa Vista and Porto Velho air bases to conduct interceptions throughout the skies of the Basin. This image of a Tucano with flaps extended and landing gear down closing in on a light plane, clearly shows why the combat jets failed in their interception missions.

groups who may cross the Brazilian borders at any given time.

An advanced datalink system allows these aircraft to fly in total electronic silence, its communications being transmitted to the R-99s and to the ground without any possibility of being intercepted. Based at Manaus, Boa Vista and Porto Velho but able to be detached to several of the region's airfields – disturbing the observation by spies on the ground – the A-29s are the claws of the SIPAM/SIVAM. They will soon be turning the skies over the Brazilian Amazon into a very uninteresting place for drug smuggling.

Which does not mean that these powerful criminal groups won't try to enter Brazil's territory through the rivers, or that they won't open clearings in the jungle for clandestine laboratories and warehouses on the Brazilian side of the border. New uncharted runways can be opened very easily adding their numbers to the hundreds already existent in the jungle. These strips make life complicated for the authorities involved in the mapping of the areas used by drug smugglers. To defeat these threats that try to hide under the canopy, the Air Force is receiving three Embraer ERJ-145RS remote sensing aircraft. Designated R-99Bs they are each fitted with a powerful MacDonald Dettwilwer IRIS synthetic aperture radar capable of generating images in 3D and of locating moving targets on the ground at ranges that reach distances of 100 kilometers. Installed under the fuselage, the radar scans the ground from great altitude. It is also capable of mapping the terrain below with much better resolution than that achieved by the commercial satellites currently being used for that task. This combination allows the R-99B to locate support bases used by the smugglers on the ground. FLIR Star Safire infrared cameras and monitoring consoles inside the R-99B will complement the equipment carried by the R-99As allowing the Brazilian Air Force to control every area

from where a threat against Brazil's sovereignty might originate. The R-99B also uses its sensors on mapping missions as there are huge portions of the Brazilian Amazon that are not covered by detailed maps. In a mere ten days, the FAB R-99Bs are capable of scanning an area of some 1.5 million square kilometers. And in a few months the whole Amazon region will have been mapped in the 1/100,000 scale, finally providing the Brazilian authorities with trustworthy maps of great portions of their country that they never possessed in such detail and thus changing a reality that has endured for centuries. The airplane's multispectral scanners, operating in bands that range from the visual to the thermal infrared will make possible the scientific analysis and observation of the environmental situation. By means of cumulative thematic maps, scientists can detect phenomena such as deforestation, pasture-clearing and accidental fires, the modification of riverbeds, effects of the increase of pollutants produced by the industries of the Northern Hemisphere over the level of ozone in the atmosphere, and the predatory occupation of the jungle.

ONE MORE STEP

Since the daring flights of the young Lieutenants from Campo dos Afonsos who had visualized the need to brave the country's outback, the Brazilian Air Force has always been present in the Amazon. Even with the outbreak of the Second World War, the Airmail Service never stopped flying to support the populations that dwell far from the urban centers. During the fifties and sixties the FAB flew to destinations far beyond the Brazilian borders and built runways nonstop. And in the closing days of the 20th Century, the Air Force has increased its presence in the region, consolidating its commitment to the most isolated inhabitants of the nation. Village names once considered exotic are now commonplace to millions of Brazilians to whom the Amazon was almost as distant as foreign countries. Little by little, the cities of the Central Plateau grew, taking an ever-larger number of people to the interior, the little jungle hamlets growing with the influx. With courage and determination, the men of the Brazilian Air Force finally launched the SIPAM/SIVAM Project, taking one step further on their mission to develop and protect the nation.

Replying to those who have long accused Brazil of attempting against the environment through the destruction of the Amazon Forest, the Government has been showing that its efforts to protect the Brazilian Amazon surpass what most other countries of the Globe expend to preserve their natural resources. At the same time, it organizes its means to disarticulate the routes used by drug smugglers over its territory. While protecting the Amazon, Brazil has begun to turn around a picture of abandon and abuse of its natural resources.

At the forefront of this great push in defending the sovereignty of the Amazon is the Brazilian Air Force. Taking development to the distant populations, integrating the nation, supplying border detachments, building runways, airfields and airports, monitoring the skies and ensuring the safety of air traffic, the Air Force continues to push Brazil towards the west, fulfilling its mission, with its wings over the Amazon.

An Embraer AT-27 Tucano belonging to the 1st/3rd Aviation Group from Boa Vista flies over a clandestine runway not far from the border. (Pages 136/137) The SIPAM/SIVAM Project is bringing a vast array of new aircraft to the Amazon. Their operation will most certainly reduce the freedom with which smuggling is conducted by air. Vectored by the R-99As, the new Embraer AT-29 ALX will be easily able to conduct interceptions of any aircraft by day or night. (Pages 138/139) Capable of carrying a heavy war load, the AT-29 will certainly be feared in the skies over the Amazon. (Pages 140/141) With the advent of the SIPAM/SIVAM, the Brazilian Air Force has arrived once and for all to the Amazon. (Pages 142/143) From the early flights of the Fledglings and WACOs of the Airmail Service, to today's capacity of defending the skies over the Amazon Basin, the Brazilian Air Force has never forgotten that its primary mission has always been to fight with its wings, for the most precious of efforts. (Page 144) Today's well being, and a better tomorrow for all Brazilians.

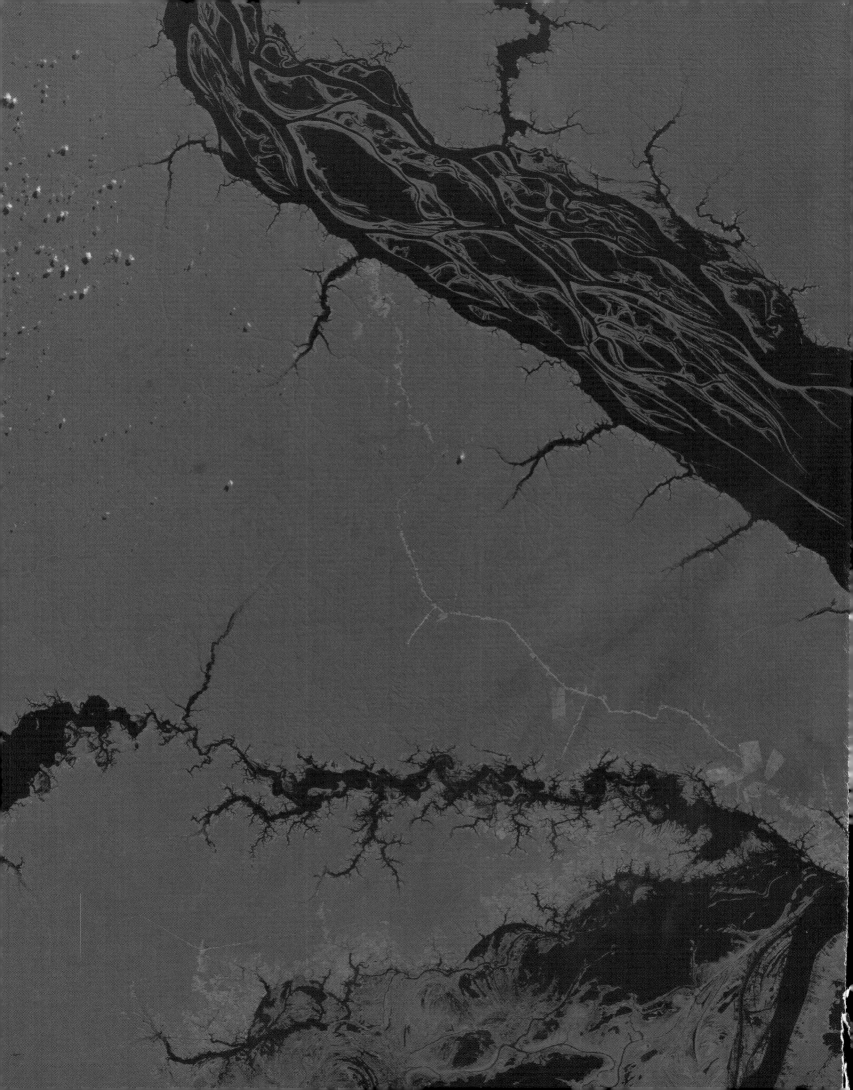